good wood finishes

ALBERT JACKSON AND DAVID DAY

GOOD WOOD FINISHES
Conceived, edited and designed at Inklink,
Greenwich, London, England

Text: Albert Jackson and David Day

Design and art direction: Simon Jennings

Project consultant: Ronnie Rustin

Text editors: Ian Kearey
and Albert Jackson

Illustrators: Robin Harris and David Day

Studio photography: Ben Jennings, Paul Chave,
and Neil Waving

Indexer: Ian Kearey

Proofreader: Mary Morton

First published in 1997
by HarperCollins Publishers, London

This paperback edition, first published in 2002
by HarperCollins Publishers, London

A CIP catalogue record is available
from the British Library

ISBN 0 00 712227 6

Printed in Singapore

Jacket design: Simon Jennings
Jacket photograph: Paul Chave
Jacket illustrations: Robin Harris and David Day

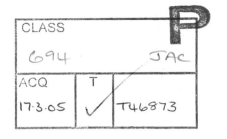

CONTENTS

INTRODUCTION

Applying a protective finish is invariably the final and arguably the most rewarding stage in any woodworking project. One can take pride in well-crafted joints, wafer-thin woodturning or intricate marquetry, but there are few delights to compare with the satisfaction of building a surface coat of polish or varnish which transforms an apparently mundane piece of wood into a uniquely beautiful object. And you don't have to be a skilled woodworker to enjoy wood finishing. It is such a varied and absorbing activity that individuals can spend years practising and perfecting their skills, so it is hardly surprising that, even in professional woodworking circles, finishing is quite often undertaken by a specialist. Similarly, a great many amateurs take up wood finishing in order to renovate inexpensive antiques for profit or merely to put new life back into much-loved heirlooms.

ACKNOWLEDGEMENTS

Consultants
The help and specialist advice provided by our technical consultants is gratefully acknowledged:

A chemist by training, **Ronnie Rustin** has a wealth of practical experience and a thorough knowledge of traditional and modern wood-finishing techniques. He is also the Managing Director of Rustins Ltd., a company famous for developing many innovative wood-finishing products. Ronnie Rustin's generous contribution to the book has been invaluable.

Tim Bizley of Touchstone Design is a professional wood grainer and marbler who has worked as a specialist decorator and muralist for over twelve years. He is also a craft-based member of the Interior Decorators and Designers Association. Tim Bizley acted as technical advisor on graining techniques and supplied all the examples of work illustrated in the chapter on wood graining.

Designer-makers
The authors and producers would like to thank the following for permission to reproduce images of their work:

John Hunnex, page 91 (CL)
Stewart Linford, page 90, 122
Paul Mathews, page 73
Wendy Maruyama, page 77
Derek Pearce, page 65 (T)
Hugh Scriven, page 39
Wales & Wales, page 40
Richard Williams, page 91 (BR)
Raymond Winkler, page 65 (BL)

Reference material and equipment
The authors and producers are grateful to the following for supplying reference and equipment used in this book:

Abrasives
CSM Trade Supplies, Brighton, East Sussex, UK
General wood finishes
Foxell & James, London EC1, UK
Langlows Products Division, Palace Chemicals Ltd., Chesham, Bucks, UK
Liberon, New Romney, Kent, UK
E. Parsons & Sons Ltd., Nailsea, Bristol, UK
Ronseal Ltd., Chapeltown, Sheffield, UK
Rustins Ltd., London, NW2, UK
Graining tools and materials
A. S. Handover Ltd., London, N1, UK
Shellac
A. F. Suter & Co. Ltd., London, E3, UK
Wm. Zinsser & Co. Inc., Somerset, NJ, USA
Spray equipment
Clarke International, London, E5, UK

Photography
The studio photographs for this book were taken by Ben Jennings, *with the following exceptions:*

Neil Waving, pages 18, 21, 22, 24 (BR), 53, 81
Paul Chave, pages 10, 32, 45, 60, 76, 80

The authors and producers also acknowledge additional photography by, and the use of photographs from, the following individuals and companies:

Robert Bosch Ltd., Uxbridge, Middlesex, page 23
Clarke International, London E5, page 82
Cuprinol Ltd., Frome, Somerset, pages 62, 64 (CL, BR)
David Day, Page 63 (T)
John Hunnex, Woodchurch, Kent, page 91 (CL)
Langlows Products Division, Palace Chemicals Ltd., Chesham Bucks, page 96
Stewart Linford Furniture (Derek St Romain), High Wycombe, Bucks, pages 90, 122
London Guildhall University (Hellena Cleary), London, E1, page 103 (C, BR, BL)
Alan Marshall, page 34
Wendy Maruyama (Cary Okazaki Studios), San Diego, California, page 77
Paul Mathews, Buckinghamshire College, High Wycombe, Bucks, page 73
Derek Pearce, London, SW 13, page 65 (T)
Ronseal Ltd., Chapeltown, Sheffield, pages 52, 91 (TR)
Sadolin UK Ltd., St Ives, Cambs, pages 47, 64 (TR)
Hugh Scriven, Shrewsbury, Shropshire, page 39
A. F. Suter & Co. Ltd., Bow London E3, page 51
Wales & Wales (Michael Hemsley FBIPP), Lewes, East Sussex, page 40
Richard Williams, Buckinghamshire College, High Wycombe, Bucks, page 91 (BR)
Raymond Winkler, Buckinghamshire College, High Wycombe, Bucks, page 65 (BL)
Shona Wood, page 63B

The authors and producers also thank the following for the use of their photographic archives:
Peter Cornish and Philip Hussey, Buckinghamshire College, High Wycombe, Bucks
John Cross, London Guildhall University, Restoration and Conservation Dept, London, E1

Key to credits
T = top, B = bottom, L = left, R = right, TL = top left, TC = top center, TR = top right, CL = center left, C = center, CR = center right, BL = bottom left, BC = bottom center, BR = bottom right

CHAPTER *1* Good-quality paint may obliterate minor imperfections, but a coat of varnish or lacquer can do nothing to improve the appearance of wood that has been inadequately prepared. The very first application of clear finish invariably exposes flaws that were completely undetectable before. Work systematically, eradicating all obvious blemishes, before sanding the wood smooth with progressively finer abrasives.

FILLING CRACKS AND HOLES

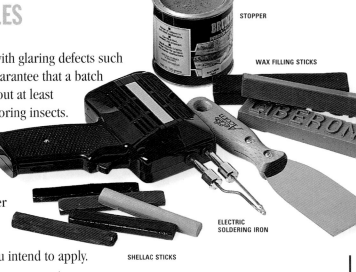

STOPPER

WAX FILLING STICKS

ELECTRIC
SOLDERING IRON

SHELLAC STICKS

Although any woodworker rejects timber with glaring defects such as end splits and shakes, it is difficult to guarantee that a batch of timber will be completely faultless, without at least some minor cracks or evidence of wood-boring insects. Try as you may to select only the better sections of the wood, you must invariably fill or patch a few cracks and holes before starting to sand to a smooth finish. However, there are a number of materials and techniques you can draw upon, depending on the dimensions of the crack or hole, and the type of finish you intend to apply.

Cellulose filler for paintwork
You can use a commercially prepared or home-made stopper when preparing wood for painting, or you can fill small holes and cracks with ordinary decorator's cellulose filler. Supplied ready-made in tubs or as a dry powder for mixing with water, cellulose filler is applied and sanded flush like wood putty.

Wood putty or stopper
Traditional filler made from wood dust mixed with glue still has its uses, but most wood finishers prefer to employ commercially prepared wood putty, or stopper, sold as a thick paste in tubes or small cans, for filling indentations. Stoppers are made in a range of colours to resemble common wood species.

Most stoppers are one-part pastes, formulated for either interior or exterior woodwork. Once set, they can be planed, sanded and drilled along with the surrounding wood; they remain slightly flexible, to absorb any subsequent movement that may be caused by the timber shrinking and expanding.

Catalysed two-part stoppers, intended primarily for larger repairs, set even harder than the standard pastes. Take care not to overfill when using them, or you may find yourself using up a great deal of sand-paper just to achieve a flush surface. Use a two-part putty if you want to build up an edge or broken corner.

Reconstituting stopper
To keep wood stopper in usable condition, replace the lid or screw cap as soon as you have taken enough for your requirements. If you find that stored water-based stopper has stiffened, try standing the tin in warm water or place the container on a radiator to make the filler pliable.

MAKING YOUR OWN STOPPER
To make your own filler, collect sawdust or, better still, the dust created by sanding a workpiece or an offcut. Mix plenty of dust with a little PVA glue to make a thick paste – a glue-rich filler tends to reject stains and polishes, creating a visible repair. As an alternative to glue, try using some of the finish you intend to apply. If colour matching proves to be a problem, try adding a drop or two of compatible stain or some powdered pigment to the mix.

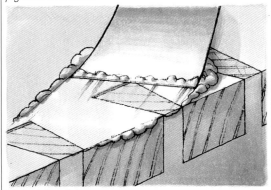

Disguising joints
Filled shoulder lines are almost always discernible, but you can make passable repairs to gappy joints that have visible end grain, using a home-made filler.

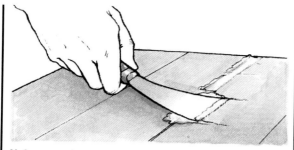

Using wood putty

Make sure the wood is clean and dry. Using a flexible filling knife, press putty into the indentations, leaving the filler slightly raised for sanding flush after it has set. Drag the knife across a crack to fill it, then smooth the putty by running the blade lengthways. Fill deep holes in stages, allowing the stopper to harden between applications.

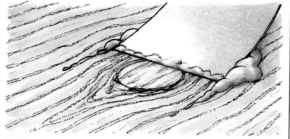

Filling large holes

Plug deep knotholes with solid wood. When the glue has set, fill gaps around the patch with wood stopper.

Colouring putty to match

To match the colour of your workpiece, make a test piece by applying stain and one finish coat to an offcut of the same wood. Select a putty that resembles the lightest background colour of the wood and, using a white ceramic tile as a palette, add compatible wood dye one drop at a time. Blend the dye into the putty with a filling knife to achieve the required tone. Mix a colour that is slightly darker than your test piece to allow for the fact that putty will be a shade lighter when dry.

Alternatively, add powdered pigments to colour the putty, plus a drop of compatible solvent if the paste becomes too stiff.

FILLING STICKS

Sticks of solidified shellac in various colours are made for melting into holes in the wood or for building up broken mouldings. Shellac can be used as a preparatory stopper for use with most surface finishes However, it may prevent an acid-catalysed cold-cure lacquer from curing properly.

Carnauba wax, mixed with pigments and resins, is ideal for plugging small wormholes. Although wax filler can be applied to bare wood that is to be French-polished or waxed, it is often best to wait until the wood is finished.

Wax sticks are made in a range of colours. If necessary, cut pieces of wax from different sticks, blending them with the tip of a soldering iron to match a specific colour. This method of filling is known as beaumontage.

Filling with shellac

Use a heated knife blade or a soldering iron to melt the tip of a shellac stick, allowing it to drip into the hole. While it is still soft, press the shellac flat with a wood chisel dipped in water. As soon as the filler hardens, pare it flush with a sharp chisel, finishing with a fine abrasive.

Using wax filling sticks

Cut off a small piece of wax and put it on a radiator to soften. Using a pocket knife, press wax into the holes. As soon as it hardens, scrape the repair flush with an old credit card. Fold a piece of sandpaper, and use the paper backing to burnish the wax filling.

PATCHING AND PLUGGING

It pays to fill a wide crack with a sliver of timber or veneer, rather than relying on stopper which could fall out. Dead knots and holes that are too large to fill successfully can be cut out and patched with solid wood. Diamond-shape patches tend to blend in better than square or rectangular ones.

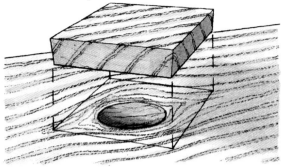

1 Cutting a diamond-shape patch
Select and cut out a diamond-shape patch from wood that matches the workpiece in grain pattern and colour. Plane a shallow bevel on all four edges of the patch.

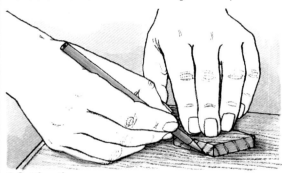

2 Cutting the recess
Hold the replacement patch over the knothole and draw round it with a pencil, then chisel out a tapered recess to receive the patch.

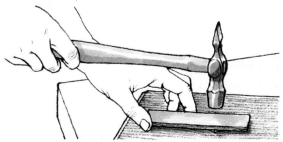

3 Inserting the patch
Tap the glued patch into the recess, cleaning off excess adhesive with a damp cloth. Leave the glue to harden, then plane flush.

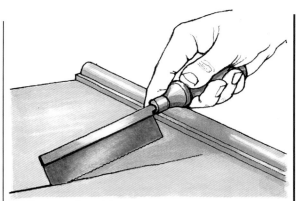

Filling cracks with veneer
Although one would never wish to buy split timber, if you are refinishing an old table top or cabinet, you may not have the choice. Enlarge a tapered crack with the tip of a dovetail saw until it is wide enough to accommodate a strip of glued veneer. When the adhesive has set, plane the repair flush.

Filling a crack with a tapered lath
To patch a wide crack or an open joint in a solid-wood panel, cut a lath from matching timber and plane a shallow bevel along both sides. Scrape any dirt and old wax polish from the crack, and tap the glued lath in place with a hammer. Plane the lath flush after the glue has set.

PLUG CUTTERS
Patch unsightly flaws with a circular patch cut with a plug cutter. These cutters are designed to exactly match holes bored with a drill bit or router cutter. You can use similar plugs to mask the sunken heads of screw fixings.

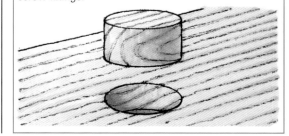

DISGUISING REPAIRS

Whether you use wood putty, shellac or solid wood to fill holes and cracks, it is often difficult to match colour and grain pattern exactly. Apply a single coat of the surface finish to see how the filling will react; if your repair is still noticeable, paint it to simulate the appearance of the surrounding wood.

Only an expert can copy grain pattern perfectly, but the aim is to fool the eye so that it is not automatically drawn to the repair. A handy trick is to paint a filled hole to look like a small knot, rather than attempt to reproduce the grain; provided the wood contains similar knots, the eye will accept the obvious difference between the patch and the background as a natural feature.

It is convenient to use artist's oil paints thinned with white spirit, but professional retouchers mix powdered pigments, available from most suppliers of wood finishes, with transparent shellac polish. Thin the polish with meths if it becomes too viscous. A white tile or a piece of glass make ideal palettes for mixing colours.

RAISING DENTS IN TIMBER

A misplaced hammer blow or an unprotected cramp head can leave an unsightly dent in an otherwise perfect surface. You could fill the dent with wood putty, but to avoid having to colour-match the repair, apply water or steam, which make the crushed wood fibres swell and lie flush with the surface.

Applying water
Using a pointed brush, drip hot water into the dent. Allow time for the wood to absorb the moisture, adding more water from time to time until the surface is flush.

Using steam
If soaking with water is unsuccessful, lay a damp cloth over the dent and apply the tip of a soldering iron to the spot. The steam generated causes the wood fibres to expand rapidly. Let the wood dry out thoroughly, then sand it smooth.

1 Painting the background colour
Using a pointed artist's paintbrush, mix pigments and shellac to approximate the palest background colour of the surrounding grain. Seal the wood, then copy the linear pattern across the patch, extending your painted grain onto the wood to blur the outline of the repair. Keep the paintwork as thin as possible.

2 Touching in darker grain
Paint in the darker flecks of grain in a similar way, softening and blending the edges to mimic actual figure. Let the shellac dry thoroughly, then protect it with another coat or two of finish. If you are using French polish, apply it lightly to avoid smudging your repair artwork.

REPAIRING VENEERS

Because they are cut so thinly, veneers are somewhat fragile until they are glued firmly to the groundwork. Even then, the occasional accident or a lack of glue can result in a raised blister or chipped veneer that has to be repaired before you can finish the work satisfactorily. The likelihood of needing to repair damaged veneer is even greater if you are restoring old furniture that has been used, and perhaps abused, for many years.

Detecting blisters

A blister usually occurs where a patch of groundwork was missed as glue was spread, prior to laying up. The blister may be obvious as soon as the work is taken out of the press, but sometimes you can only detect a patch of loose veneer by tapping the surface with your finger-tips; a change in sound from that of solid, adhered veneer denotes a blister.

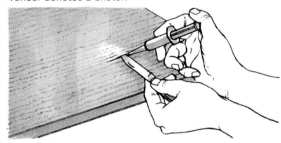

1 Injecting glue

In order to introduce glue beneath the veneer, dampen the blister and slit it lengthways with a sharp knife. Work some PVA glue through the slit with the knife blade or, better still, inject some with a plastic syringe.

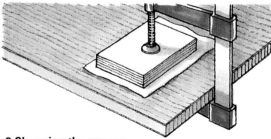

2 Clamping the veneer

Press the blister flat to squeeze out air and glue, wiping surplus adhesive from the surface with a damp cloth. Lay a small piece of polythene over the repair and clamp it down, using a block of scrap wood to spread the load. After the glue has set, remove traces of glue with sandpaper or a cabinet scraper.

Removing a foreign body

A speck of coarse sawdust or a piece of grit trapped beneath veneer will form a blister that cannot be pressed flat until the foreign body is extricated. Wet the patch thoroughly and cut a V-shape flap in the vicinity of the blister. Peel back the flap and scrape out the speck with a knife blade. Brush some glue onto the groundwork and clamp down the veneer.

PRESSING OLD VENEER

Until comparatively recently, veneer was invariably laid using animal glue. Although in many ways it is the ideal glue for veneering, animal glue is not water-proof, and veneer is prone to buckling if moisture is able to penetrate, perhaps through a hairline crack. One of the great advantages of animal glue is that it can be softened with heat and the veneer pressed down without having to slit the blister to introduce fresh adhesive.

Ironing a blister

Place a piece of brown paper over the blistered veneer and apply a warm iron, gradually flattening the veneer as the glue softens. Although you can accelerate the process by substituting a damp cloth for the paper, the steam will spoil the surface finish; however, this may not be a problem if you are in the process of re-polishing.

Patching veneer

It is relatively easy to cut out a flaw, such as a knot hole or cigarette burn, and insert a patch of veneer. Provided you are repairing new work, it should be possible to find a piece of veneer that is identical in thickness, with closely matched grain pattern and colour.

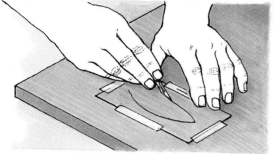

1 Cutting a patch

Tape the piece of veneer over the blemish, aligning the grain, and trace a boat-shape patch with a sharp knife. Cut through both layers, down to the groundwork.

2 Removing the waste

Lay the patch aside and cut out the waste with a wood chisel to reveal the groundwork. Scrape the groundwork clean, then glue and clamp the patch in place.

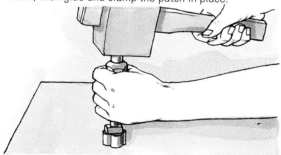

Using a veneer punch

Special punches, with wavy cutting edges, are made for stamping patches out of thin sheets of veneer. Holding the punch upright, give it one firm blow with a mallet to cut an irregular-shape patch from your chosen veneer. Place the punch over the flaw and cut out an identical recess for the patch.

Repairing chipped veneer

Unless the edge of a veneered panel is lipped with solid wood, the unprotected veneer is very vulnerable. If you accidentally chip the edge, repair it immediately with glue before the sliver of veneer gets swept away. If you are restoring old veneer, insert a patch to disguise the damage.

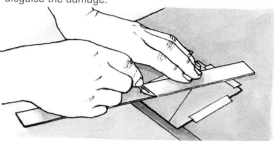

1 Trimming the veneer

Tape down a small piece of veneer so that it just overhangs the chipped edge, and cut a V-shape patch through both layers. Make sure you don't score the groundwork too deeply.

2 Paring down to the groundwork

Carefully pare out waste, and scrape the groundwork with a wood chisel to leave a clean recess. Tape the glued patch in place and clamp it down, using a layer of polythene to prevent the softening block from sticking to the work.

3 Trimming the overlap

When the glue has set, turn the work face-down and trim the patch flush with the edge of the panel. Sand the top surface and touch in the grain as required (see page 13).

ABRASIVES

The surfaces of wood must be brought to as near-perfect a finish as possible before beginning to apply varnish, lacquer or any other clear coating. Rubbing wood smooth with abrasives is the usual way of getting the desired result, and woodworkers are today presented with an enormous range of products to achieve their aims.

Not only is the wood itself smoothed with abrasives, but each coat of finish is also rubbed over lightly, to remove specks of dust and other debris that become embedded as the finish sets.

Although sandpaper as such is no longer manufactured, the term is still used to describe all forms of abrasive, and we still 'sand' wood by hand and with power tools. Most abrasives are now manufactured using synthetic materials that are far superior to the sandpaper of old.

The structure of modern abrasives

An abrasive for woodworking is made by gluing irregular particles of natural or synthetic grit to a backing sheet, usually of paper or cloth. The efficiency, or the rate at which the abrasive wears away the wood, depends on several factors: the size of the particles and the ability of the material to retain its cutting edges; the degree to which the sandpaper can resist clogging with wood dust and sticky resins; and the quality of the bond between grit and backing, without which the particles become detached and are swept away.

Abrasive materials

You can choose from a number of abrasive grits, depending on their relative costs and the nature of the material you are finishing.

Crushed glass is used to make inexpensive abrasive paper, intended primarily for sanding softwood that is to be painted. When compared with other abrasives, glass is fairly soft and wears rapidly. Glasspaper can be recognized easily by its sand-like colour.

Garnet is a natural mineral which, when crushed, produces relatively hard particles with sharp cutting edges. It has the added advantage that the grains tend to fracture before they become dull, presenting fresh cutting edges – in effect, they are self-sharpening. Reddish-brown garnet paper is used by cabinetmakers for sanding softwoods and hardwoods.

SELF-LUBRICATING
SILICON CARBIDE SILICON CARBIDE GARNET

Aluminium oxide is used to manufacture a great many abrasive products for sanding by hand and with power tools. Available in a number of different colours, aluminium oxide is especially suitable for sanding dense hardwoods to a fine finish.

Silicon carbide is the hardest and most expensive woodworking abrasive. It is an excellent material for sanding hardwoods, MDF and chipboard, but it is most often used for manufacturing abrasive paper and cloth for rubbing down between coats of varnish and paint. Water is used as a lubricant when smoothing finishes with black to dark-grey 'wet-and-dry' paper. A pale-grey, self-lubricating paper is available for rubbing down finishes that would be harmed by water.

ALUMINIUM-OXIDE

1 Paper- or cloth-backed rolls
Economical and ideal for sanding turned legs and spindles.

2 Slashed cloths
They can be crumpled in the hand and applied to work on the lathe.

3 Velour-backed strips
Peel-off strips for sanding blocks and power sanders.

CRUSHED GLASS

Backing
The backing is basically nothing more than a vehicle that carries the grit to the work. Nevertheless, the choice of backing material can be crucial to the performance of the abrasive.

Paper is the cheapest backing material used in the manufacture of woodworking abrasives. It is available in a range of thicknesses or 'weights' – flexible lightweight papers are ideal for sanding by hand, although medium-weight backing is perhaps better for wrapping round a sanding block. Thicker papers are used with power sanders. Paper backings are designated by letter, according to their thickness or flexibility, ranging from A, the lightest, to F.

Cloth or woven-textile backings provide very tough and durable, yet flexible, abrasive products. You can crease a good cloth backing without it cracking, splitting or shedding its grit. Cloth makes ideal belts for power sanders and strips for smoothing turned spindles.

Non-woven nylon-fibre pads, impregnated with aluminium-oxide or silicon-carbide grains, are ideal for rubbing down finishes and for applying wax polish and oil. The large cavities within the pad will not become clogged, and it can be washed out under running water. The abrasive coating extends throughout the thickness of a pad so that, as the fibres get worn away, fresh abrasive is exposed. Abrasive belts, rolls and discs are all made with nylon-fibre backing.

Nylon fibre is frequently used for stripping old finishes (see page 33), and, because it does not rust, it is ideal for applying water-based products. Nylon-fibre pads are safe to use on oak, which is prone to staining when minute particles from steel wool get caught in its open grain.

Non-abrasive polishing pads make excellent applicators for wood dyes, oils and wax polishes.

Foamed plastic is used as a secondary backing when you need to spread even pressure over a contoured surface. You can buy paper-backed silicon-carbide glued to thin sponges, for rubbing down varnished mouldings, turned legs or spindles.

4 Foam-backed pads
Flexible pads follow the contours of a workpiece.

6 Standard-size sheets
Sandpaper or cloth sheets measure 280 x 230mm (11 x 9in).

5 Non-woven pads
Nylon fibre impregnated with abrasive material.

7 Flexible-foam pads
Ideal for sanding mouldings.

Bond

The bond, or method of gluing abrasives to the backing, is vital, both in ensuring that the grit stays put, and because it affects the characteristics of sandpaper.

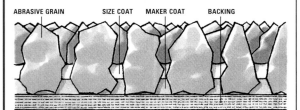

ABRASIVE GRAIN   SIZE COAT   MAKER COAT   BACKING

As the abrasive particles are embedded in the first, or maker, coat of adhesive, an electrostatic charge orientates each grain so that it stands perpendicular to the backing, with its sharp cutting edges uppermost. A second layer of adhesive, known as the size coat, is sprayed onto the abrasive to anchor the grains and provide lateral support.

Animal glue, which softens with heat generated by sanding, is used when flexibility is a requirement. Resin, on the other hand, is heat-resistant, making it ideal for power sanding. Because it is waterproof, resin is also used for the manufacture of wet-and-dry papers. A combination of adhesives modifies the properties of a paper. Resin over glue, for example, would make a relatively heat-resistant paper that would be more flexible than a resin-over-resin combination.

Additives

A third coating of stearate, a powdered soap, packs the spaces between the grains, presenting a finer abrasive surface to the work and reducing premature clogging with wood dust. Stearate, and other chemical additives, act as dry lubricants for abrasives used for rubbing down coats of hard finish.

Antistatic additives in the size coat reduce clogging dramatically and increase the efficiency of dust extractors. This leads to a decrease in dust deposits on the work, surrounding surfaces and power tools – a distinct advantage when you may have to sand work-pieces and apply finishes in the same workshop.

Storing abrasives

Wrap sandpaper or cloth in plastic to protect it from damp or humid conditions. Store sheets flat, and don't let the abrasive surfaces rub together.

GRADING SANDPAPER

Sandpapers are graded according to particle size, and are categorized as extra-fine, fine, medium, coarse or extra-coarse. For most purposes, these classifications are adequate but, should you want to work through a series of precisely graded abrasives, each category is subdivided by number. There are several different grading systems in operation, none of which make for exact comparison. However, as the chart below demonstrates, you can safely assume that the higher the number, the finer the grit.

Sandpaper grades		
Extra-coarse	50	1
	60	½
Coarse	80	0
	100	2/0
Medium	120	3/0
	150	4/0
	180	5/0
Fine	220	6/0
	240	7/0
	280	8/0
Extra-fine	320	9/0
	360	-
	400	-
	500	-
	600	-

Closed or open coat

Sandpapers are also categorized according to the density of grit. A closed-coat sandpaper, with densely packed abrasive grains, cuts relatively quickly, as it has a great many cutting edges for a given area. An open-coat sandpaper has larger spaces between the grains, which reduces clogging and is more suitable for resinous softwoods.

SANDING BY HAND

Most woodworkers resort to power sanding in the early stages of preparing a workpiece, but it is usually necessary to finish by hand, especially if the work includes mouldings. You can, of course, do the whole thing by hand – it just takes longer.

Always sand parallel to the grain, working from coarser to finer grits so that each application removes the scratches left by the previous paper or cloth. Stroking abrasives across the grain leaves scratches that are difficult to remove.

You will find it easier to sand most components before assembly, but take care not to round over the shoulders of a joint or create a slack fit by removing too much wood. Restoring old furniture presents additional problems of sanding up to corners and of possibly sanding cross grain where one component meets another.

Sanding flat surfaces
Stand beside the bench so that you can rub a sanding block in straight strokes, parallel with the grain; sweeping your arm in an arc tends to leave cross-grain scratches. Work at a steady pace, letting the abrasive do the work. It pays to change the paper frequently, rather than tiring yourself by rubbing harder to achieve the same ends.

Cover the surface evenly, keeping the block flat on the wood at all times, especially as you approach the edges of the work, or you may inadvertently round over sharp corners.

Sanding end grain
Before sanding, stroke end grain with your fingers to determine the direction of fibre growth. It will feel smoother in one direction than the other; to achieve the best finish, sand in the smoothest direction.

SANDING BLOCKS
It is much easier to sand a flat surface evenly if you wrap a piece of abrasive paper around a sanding block. You can make your own from an offcut of wood with a piece of cork tile glued to the underside, but this is hardly worth the trouble when factory-made cork or rubber sanding blocks are so cheap.

Most blocks are designed to be wrapped with a piece of sandpaper torn from a standard sheet, but you can buy sanding blocks that take ready-cut self-adhesive or velour-backed strips of abrasive that are peeled off when they need replacing. Double-sided blocks are made with firm plastic foam on one side, for sanding flat surfaces, and a softer sponge on the reverse, for mouldings and curved profiles.

Velcro-lined   Double-sided   Cork   Rubber
foam plastic

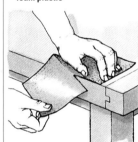

Tearing sandpaper
Fold a sheet of sandpaper over the edge of a bench, and tear it into strips that fit your sanding block. Wrap a piece of the paper around the sole of the block, gripping the sides with fingers and thumb.

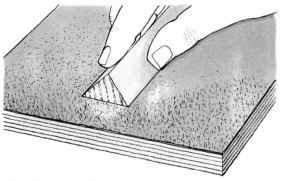

Sanding small items
It is impossible to clamp and sand small items using conventional methods. Instead, glue a sheet of sandpaper face-up on a flat board and rub the workpiece across the abrasive.

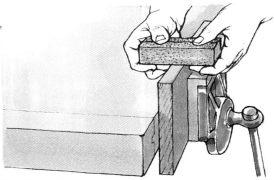

Sanding edges

It is even more difficult to retain sharp corners when sanding narrow edges. To keep the block level, clamp the work upright in a vice and, holding the block at each end, run your fingertips along each side of the work as you rub the abrasive back and forth. Finally, stroke the block lightly along the corner to remove the arris and prevent splinters.

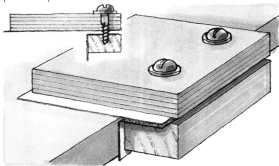

Making an edge-sanding block

It is especially important to sand edges accurately when working on edge-veneered boards. Screw together two pieces of wood to make an edge-sanding block, trapping two pieces of sandpaper face-to-face between them. Fold back one piece of paper to form a right angle. Rub the block along the edge of the work, simultaneously sanding both adjacent surfaces.

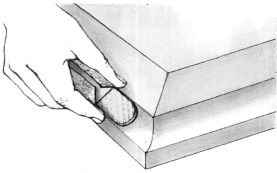

Sanding mouldings

Wrap sandpaper around a shaped block or dowel when sanding mouldings. Alternatively, use foam-backed paper or an impregnated nylon-fibre pad.

SANDING SEQUENCE

Every woodworker develops his or her preferred sequence for preparing a workpiece for finishing, but the following will serve as a guide to suitable grades of abrasive to achieve the result. You may need to experiment and modify the sequence when dealing with different woods. Sanding a close-grain hardwood with an extra-fine abrasive, for example, tends to burnish the surface, making it more difficult to apply wood dye subsequently.

Start with 120 grit aluminium-oxide or garnet paper followed by 180 grit, until the surface appears smooth and free from tool marks and similar blemishes. You only need to resort to anything as coarse as 80 to 100 grit if the wood is not already planed to a reasonably smooth surface.

Remove the dust between sandings, using a tack rag – a sticky cloth designed for picking up dust and fine debris. If you fail to keep the work clean, abrasive particles shed during the previous sanding may leave relatively deep scratches in the surface.

Sand again for no more than 30 to 60 seconds, using 220 grit, then raise the grain by wiping the surface with a damp cloth. Wait for 10 to 20 minutes, by which time the moisture will have caused the minute wood fibres to expand and stand proud of the surface. Lightly skim the surface with a fresh piece of 220 abrasive to remove these 'whiskers', leaving a perfectly smooth surface. It is particularly important to raise grain before applying water-based products.

At this stage, you can safely apply a surface finish, but if you feel the workpiece demands an extra-special finish, raise the grain once more and rub down very lightly, using 320 grit paper or an impregnated nylon-fibre pad.

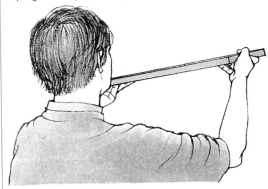

Checking a sanded surface

Inspect the workpiece against the light at a shallow angle, to check that the surface is sanded evenly and that you have removed all obvious scratches.

POWER SANDING

Nowadays, portable sanding machines relieve the woodworker from the tiresome chore of sanding for long periods, but even orbital sanders are apt to leave tiny whorls or scratches on the wood that show up only after the first coat of finish is applied. As a safeguard, raise the grain with a damp cloth after you have finished power sanding, and rub over lightly by hand, using a fine abrasive paper or nylon-fibre pad.

Belt sander

Belt sanders

These are heavy-duty power sanders that are capable of reducing even sawn timber to a smooth finish. As a result, they remove a great deal of wood very quickly, and have to be carefully controlled to avoid rounding over the edges of a workpiece or wearing through a layer of veneer. Special accessories that frame the sanding bed are helpful in preventing the tool from tilting, especially as you approach the edge of a panel. Belt sanding creates a great deal of dust, so fit a collecting bag or use an extractor (see page 24).

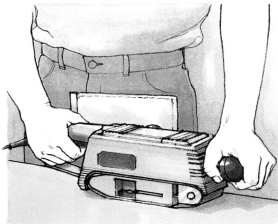

Using a belt sander

There are few occasions when you would need a belt sander for fine woodwork, but it is useful for smoothing large baulks of timber or some man-made boards. Switch on and gradually lower the sander onto the work. As soon as you make contact, move the sander forward – allowing the tool to remain stationary or dropping it heavily onto the surface will score the wood deeply. Sand in the direction of the grain only, keeping the tool moving and using parallel overlapping strokes. Lift the sander off the work before switching off.

Sanding belts

Cloth- and paper-backed belts are made for the average 60 to 100mm (2⅜ to 4in) wide sanders. They are held taut between two rollers, the front one being adjustable to control tension and tracking. Operating a lever releases the tension so that you can change a belt; once the sander is running, adjust a small knob to centre the belt on the rollers. Use medium-to-fine abrasive belts for most applications.

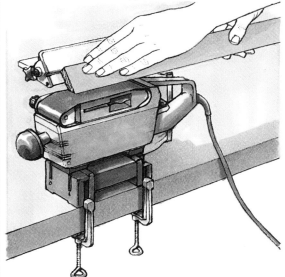

Fixed belt sanders

Using a purpose-made cramp, you can attach a portable belt sander upside-down on a bench, allowing you to sand small components by applying them to the moving belt. You can use a fence to guide the work, and you can shape curved workpieces over the end roller.

Orbital sanders

Provided you work through a series of progressively finer abrasives (see page 20) and take the trouble to raise the grain before the final light sanding, an orbital sander will produce a surface that, to all intents and purposes, is ready for finishing. Before applying a clear finish, however, always inspect the surface carefully to make sure there are no swirling scratches caused by the elliptical motion of the base plate. Some orbital sanders can be switched to a straight reciprocal stroke to eliminate this possibility.

Orbital sander

Palm-grip sander

Perforating sandpaper

Ready-made sheets are very convenient, but you can make considerable cost savings by perforating plain sandpaper strips or rolls. Using a soft pencil and white paper, make a rubbing of the perforations in your sander's base plate. Use it as a pattern for drilling matching holes in a piece of MDF, and glue into them short lengths of pointed dowel rod.

Attach a strip of abrasive to the base plate, and then press your sander down onto your perforator to pierce the sandpaper.

Palm-grip sanders

The majority of orbital sanders are designed to be held in both hands, but lightweight, palm-grip sanders are also available.

Sanding sheets

Strips of sandpaper are made specifically for use with orbital sanders. Designated as half, third and quarter sheets, their proportions are based on the standard-size sheets made for hand-sanding (see page 17). They are held in place by a wire clamp at each end of the sander's base plate; alternatively, strips are velour-lined or self-adhesive for easy replacement. To preserve your health and reduce clogging, choose a sander that incorporates dust extraction; the base plate and sandpaper are both perforated so that dust is sucked directly from beneath the tool into a collecting bag or vacuum cleaner (see page 24).

Using orbital sanders

Don't apply excessive pressure to an orbital sander, as this tends to overheat the abrasive, causing dust and resin to clog the grit prematurely. A sensation of pins and needles in your fingers after prolonged sanding indicates that you are pressing too hard.

Keep the tool moving back and forth with the grain, covering the surface as evenly as possible. If you are using a variable-speed sander, select the slowest rate for coarser grits and gradually increase the speed as you progress with finer abrasives.

Cordless sanders

There are obvious advantages to be gained from using a battery-powered sander: there's no electrical flex to get caught up on the workpiece, and you can work outside if you wish, completely independent of a mains supply. However, only a few cordless sanders are currently available.

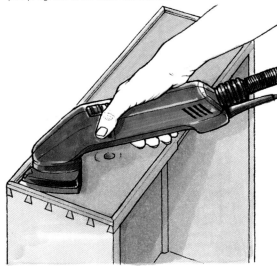

Sanding into corners

With a well-designed orbital sander, it should be possible to sand into right angles and up to the ends of fixed rails or panels. However, for really tight corners and cross-grain mitres, use a delta sander, which has a triangular base plate.

RANDOM-ORBITAL SANDERS

The combined rotational and eccentric motions of a random-orbital sander practically eliminate discernible scratches on a wood surface. The circular base plate takes sanding discs, along with the usual options – Velcro or self-adhesive attachment, and perforations for dust extraction. Some sanders can cope with flat and curved surfaces, while others have interchangeable base plates so that you can increase the sanding area for working on large boards or panels. The only disadvantage is that you cannot sand into corners (see left).

23

Disc sanders

With the exception of bench-mounted machines, cabinetmakers seldom use disc sanders, which can score deep scratches in the wood. However, wood-turners employ the combined actions of disc sander and lathe to their advantage for sanding bowls and platters.

Flexible-shaft sanders and discs

Arbor-mounted foam pads, from 25 to 75mm (1 to 3in) in diameter, are made for use in portable power drills or, better still, highly manoeuvrable, flexible-shaft sanders. Velour-lined or self-adhesive abrasive discs, with cloth or paper backing, come ready-made to fit every size of foam pad.

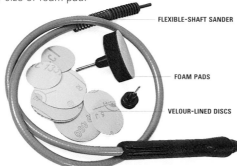

FLEXIBLE-SHAFT SANDER

FOAM PADS

VELOUR-LINED DISCS

Advantages for woodturners

Miniature disc sanders are ideal for intricate woodwork such as carving or modelmaking, but they are especially suited to woodturners, because the soft-foam pads conform to the changing contours of a wooden bowl or vase, ensuring an even distribution of pressure without generating too much heat. More importantly, since both the disc and workpiece rotate simultaneously, you can remove tool marks rapidly without scratching the wood.

Bench-mounted sanders

A relatively large-diameter metal disc sander, mounted rigidly to the bench, is perfect for finishing end grain. Using coarse to fine grits, you can also shape work-pieces with a disc sander. Keep the workpiece moving, and press the end grain lightly against the downward-rotating side of the disc. Applying excessive pressure invariably scorches the wood.

PROTECTING YOURSELF FROM DUST

Power sanders are not especially dangerous, provided they are used with care. However, the dust generated by sanding can be very injurious to health, and may also constitute a fire hazard.

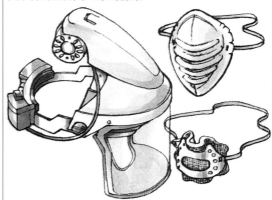

Face masks and helmets

At the very least, make sure you wear a face mask to cover your nose and mouth when sanding. Cheap disposable masks are available from any tool store, and are usually supplied as part of the kit when you hire power sanders.

A battery-powered respirator, built into a light-weight helmet, offers the ultimate protection. A stream of filtered air, blown behind the transparent face screen, prevents you breathing airborne dust.

Dust extractors

Good-quality power sanders are fitted with an extractor port that discharges dust into a bag, for disposal after work or when the bag is full. For greater efficiency, attach a sander to an industrial vacuum cleaner that sucks the dust directly from the work surface. A purpose-made extractor is activated as you switch on the sander.

SCRAPING WOOD

Even though sanding is the most-used method for smoothing timber, scraping the surface, which removes minute shavings instead of dust particles, produces a superior finish. Because a scraper can take such a fine cut, you can use it on areas of wild grain that are difficult to plane well.

Controlling a cabinet scraper
Holding the scraper in both hands, lean it away from you and push the tool forwards. Bending a scraper, by pressing with your thumbs near the bottom edge, concentrates the forces in a narrow band, so that you can scrape small blemishes from the wood. By experimenting with different curvatures and angles, you can vary the action and cutting depth to suit the particular task.

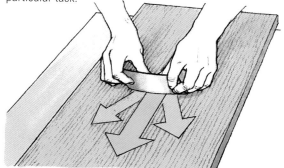

Levelling wood panels
To scrape a panel flat and level, work in two directions at a slight angle to the general direction of grain. To finish, smooth the wood by scraping parallel with the grain. Use a similar method when scraping out small patches of dried glue or scorching, to avoid leaving a deep hollow.

Cabinet scrapers
The standard cabinet scraper is nothing more than a small rectangle of tempered steel. For shaped surfaces and mouldings, you need a scraper with a pair of curved edges, or a goose-neck scraper that is shaped to accommodate a great many convex and concave radii. Before using a scraper, you must prepare and sharpen its cutting edges.

1 Filing a scraper
Clamp the scraper in a bench vice and draw-file its two long edges to make them perfectly square. To prevent the file rocking, steady it by running your fingertips against each face of the scraper.

2 Honing the scraper
Filing leaves rough edges that must be rubbed down with an oiled slipstone. Keep the stone flat on the faces of the scraper, and rub it along both sides of each cutting edge.

3 Raising a burr
Stretch the metal along both cutting edges with a smooth metal burnisher. If you can't get the proper tool, use the curved back of a gouge. Holding the scraper on the bench top, strop each edge firmly four or five times, drawing the burnisher towards you while keeping it flat on the scraper.

4 Turning the burr
For the scraper to function, the raised burrs must be folded over at right angles. Holding the burnisher at a slight angle to the burred edge, draw the tool firmly along the scraper two or three times.

FILLING AND SEALING GRAIN

An open-grain timber, such as oak or ash, looks good when coated with a satin varnish or oil, but when French polish or gloss varnish sinks into each pore, the result is a speckled, pitted surface that detracts from the quality of the finish.

Perhaps the ideal solution is to apply coat after coat of the finish itself, rubbing down between applications until the pores are filled flush, but this is a slow, laborious process, which is why the majority of woodworkers opt for a ready-mixed grain filler. Most general-purpose fillers are thick wood-colour pastes. Choose a colour that closely resembles the species you are finishing, always erring on the darker side when a perfect match is impossible.

1 Applying grain filler
Make sure the surface is completely clean and dust-free. Dip a pad of coarse burlap into the grain filler and rub it vigorously into the wood, using over-lapping circular strokes.

2 Removing excess filler
Before the paste dries completely, wipe across the grain with clean burlap to remove excess filler from the surface. Use a pointed stick to remove paste embedded in mouldings or carving.

3 Rubbing down
Leave the grain filler to dry thoroughly overnight, then sand lightly in the direction of the grain, using 220 grit, self-lubricating silicon-carbide paper. Rub down mouldings or turned pieces with an abrasive nylon-fibre pad.

Filling stained timber
It is debatable whether it is better to colour the wood before or after grain filling. To fill first may result in patchy, uneven colour, but if you apply filler over stained timber, there is the possibility that you may wear through the colour when sanding at a later stage. One solution is to stain the timber first, then protect it with sanding sealer, or two coats of transparent French polish, before applying a grain filler mixed with some of the same compatible wood dye.

SANDING SEALER
Sealing serves more than one purpose. On porous woods it prevents the finish being absorbed, just as a primer does for paint, and can be used as the first base coat for French polish. Perhaps most important of all, shellac-based sanding sealer makes an excellent barrier coat, preventing wood stains being re-dissolved and also sealing in contaminants, such as silicone oil, that affect the setting of the final finish. For this reason, it often makes sense to seal old furniture that has been stripped prior to refinishing (see page 33). However, since sanding sealer prevents some varnishes from setting satisfactorily, check the manufacturer's instructions before starting.

Applying sanding sealer
Sand the work well and pick up the dust with a tack rag. Brush sanding sealer onto the wood and leave it to dry for an hour or two. Rub the surface with fine sandpaper, an abrasive pad, or 0000-grade steel wool before applying your chosen finish. You may need a second sealing coat on very porous timber.

CHAPTER 2 Most experts agree that when it comes to restoring nicely aged wood finishes, it is best to do as little as possible, erring on the side of preservation rather than renewal. The subtle shading of colour and tone – the patina of antique finishes – is all too easily lost, yet so very difficult to replicate.

REPAIRING FINISHES

CLEANING OLD FINISHES

Over a prolonged period of use, a piece of furniture or a wooden utensil gradually collects a layer of dirty wax polish or oil that masks the colour and grain pattern. Just as we become used to the appearance of a painting obscured by discoloured varnish, it may be hard to imagine how a finish may once have looked and how much of an improvement can be made. However, it is safe to say that most old pieces benefit from cleaning and, in some cases, this is all that is required to restore the quality of a finish.

Cleaning fluids
There are a number of preparations on the market that dissolve accumulated layers of grime, but ordinary white spirit is perfectly adequate.

1 Applying cleaning fluid
Dip a pad of burlap or 000-grade steel wool into the fluid, and rub the dirty wood in the direction of the grain. A liquid slurry of cleaner and dissolved wax forms on the surface; wipe it off with a clean cloth pad or paper towel before it congeals.

2 Cleaning mouldings
Use steel wool or an abrasive nylon pad to clean out crevices, corners and mouldings where wax and dirt tend to collect most thickly. Don't rub too hard in case you should wear through the finish on high points. Finally, clean all surfaces with a soft cloth or a non-abrasive polishing pad (see page 17) dipped in white spirit.

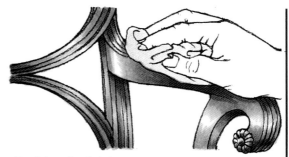

3 Reviving the finish
The combined action of white spirit and abrasives leaves the original finish looking clean but lacking vitality. You can buy proprietary creams and emulsions to burnish the surface, or use any liquid abrasive, such as metal polish or car-paint cleaner. Pour some onto a soft-cloth pad and rub the matt surface vigorously to restore its glossy finish, then apply a light dressing of wax polish.

Don't use a burnishing cream or liquid if you have stripped a wax finish down to the bare wood.

PATCHING THE FINISH
Burnishing alone may not be sufficient to restore badly worn or scuffed areas of a finish. Whatever the finish, it is possible to use wax polish to restore the colour locally but, if there are very thin patches that need rebuilding, you need to identify the original polish or varnish.

Identifying the finish
Any piece made around the turn of the century is probably French-polished; check by rubbing an inconspicuous area with a white cloth dampened with meths, wrapped round your fingers. French polish will stain the cloth brown, but if you are picking up nothing but surface dust make a similar test for cellulose lacquer using the appropriate thinner. Cellulose thinner will also dissolve acrylic varnishes but, since these finishes were not available until quite recently, the age of the piece should give you a clue. Most modern varnishes are completely insoluble in anything other than a purpose-made chemical stripper.

REMOVING SCRATCHES

You would be hard-pressed to find a piece of furniture that has seen years of service without getting scratched to some degree, and most of the time we are content to ignore this type of superficial damage. However, it's a different story when you accidentally drag a sharp object across a newly polished surface. Only an expert can hope to make scratches invisible, but there are ways to render them less conspicuous, depending on the severity of the damage. Treat deep scratches individually, filling them flush with wax or some of the original finish. On the other hand, it's better to burnish out minor scratches or blend them into the background colour.

Burnishing a scratched surface
Burnish out fine scratches with an abrasive reviver (see page 28). Don't persist for too long; it is better to disguise scratches rather than risk wearing through the polish in an attempt to eradicate them altogether.

Disguising hairline scratches
Surface scratches are pale in colour, and tend to stand out more than blemishes that are darker in tone. Conceal a mass of fine scratches by rubbing over the damaged area with a proprietary scratch cover, a liquid blend of waxes and colouring agents.

Retouching scratches
Touch in individual scratches with a special felt-tip pen filled with wood dye. Ten minutes later, you can dress the surface with a coat of shellac or wax polish.

Filling with wax sticks
Sets of coloured-wax sticks are sold for filling relatively deep scratches. Rub the sharp edge of a stick across the scratch until it is filled flush, adjusting the colour with other sticks until you achieve a close match. If your workshop is cold, warm the sticks very slightly before using them. Smooth the deposit and wipe excess wax from the surface with a soft cloth, then cover the repair with a light dressing of wax polish.

ADDING SHELLAC POLISH OR VARNISH
Professional restorers melt stick shellac (see page 11) into deep scratches, but it takes practice to avoid overfilling and perhaps creating a repair that is larger than the original flaw. A slower but more controllable process is to fill the scratch with ordinary shellac polish (see pages 52–3) that has been poured into a shallow dish and left exposed to the air to thicken slightly. Employ a similar technique, using varnish straight from the can to repair a modern finish.

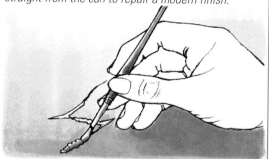

Filling with shellac polish
Using a fine artist's paintbrush, run some thickened polish along the scratch and let it set. If necessary, add more polish until it just stands proud of the surface, then leave it to harden thoroughly. Wrap fine self-lubricating silicon-carbide paper around a very small cork block, and use it to sand the repair flush. Burnish the surface with a liquid finish reviver (see opposite) or wax polish.

ERADICATING STAINS

Disfiguring stains, in the form of white rings or dark patches, are often found on old tables and sideboards. They are invariably caused by water or alcohol being left to etch the surface of the finish, most usually French polish. Very little water or alcohol is required to do the damage. Ring stains are typically the result of moisture trapped beneath a flower vase or tumbler. A mug of coffee or a hot plate will have a similar effect, but this damage usually goes deeper.

In every case, the problem is soluble without having to refinish the piece, provided the moisture has not penetrated to the wood itself and left a dark patch. Your only solution then is to strip the finish and bleach out the stain.

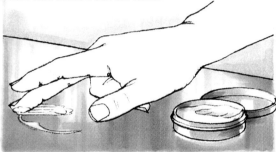

Smearing with petroleum jelly
Smear a white patch liberally with petroleum jelly and leave it to soak in for 24 hours. Wipe off excess jelly with a soft cloth and, provided the damage was not too severe, the stain will have disappeared.

Wiping with methylayed spirit
Since French polish is soluble in methylated spirit, it is sometimes possible to 'pull over' a white stain. Moisten a soft cloth pad with meths (see page 57) and wipe it lightly across the stain. Make sure the cloth is never more than damp, or there is a very real risk of spoiling the finish. Leave the meths to evaporate, then repeat the treatment until the stain disappears.

Burnishing stains
Whatever the finish, you can burnish out white rings with a proprietary finish reviver, liquid metal polish, or car-paint cleaner on a pad of soft cloth. Having removed the stain, burnish the rest of the surface lightly to an even finish, then dress it with a coat of wax or French polish.

BLEACHING STAINS

Crazing or hairline cracks allow moisture to seep below the finish, where it stains the wood, forming dark irregular patches. Your only recourse in this situation is to strip the finish from the surface (see pages 32–5) and bleach out the stain with a solution of oxalic acid. Specialist wood-finishing suppliers stock oxalic-acid crystals, or you may be able to buy them from your local pharmacist. Oxalic acid is extremely toxic and must be stored out of the reach of children.

Ventilate the workspace when mixing and using wood bleaches, and wear protective gloves, goggles, and an apron. Half-fill a glass jar with warm water and gradually add crystals, stirring with a wooden spatula until no more will dissolve. Never pour water onto oxalic-acid crystals.

Applying the bleach
Leave the solution to stand for about 10 minutes, then paint it onto the stain, using a white-fibre or nylon brush. Let the wood dry, then apply more bleach if the stain persists. Finally wash the wood with water and leave it to dry thoroughly. Wearing a face mask, sand the raised grain with fine abrasive paper. Dispose of any remaining solution safely.

STRIPPING FINISHES

Purists would argue that you should never strip an old finish, because the colour and general patina of the original polish add greatly to the value of antique furniture. In principle, this is good advice, and it would certainly be counterproductive to refinish a valuable table or cabinet simply to brighten it up, but there are circumstances that leave you with few alternatives.

Fire or water damage, for example, can be so severe that the original finish is irretrievably damaged, so you lose nothing by stripping it. Also, you will have to remove a finish if you need to bleach out small stains, but in this case strip just enough polish to make the repair and the refinishing as straightforward as possible.

Remember that not all old furniture is valuable, and that stripping and refinishing may make it more serviceable. Similarly, built-in cupboards may benefit from stripping if you are to make a decent job of redecorating.

Having decided that stripping is appropriate, there are a number of alternative methods and materials to consider. Your final decision will rest on factors such as the type of finish to be removed, the size and quality of the workpiece and, to some extent, cost and convenience.

1 Panelled doors
Painted cupboard doors can usually be stripped safely in a chemical dip (see page 34), but a hot-caustic dip may split thin panels.

2 Solid-wood chairs
Another potential candidate for industrial stripping, especially as having to strip by hand a number of chairs with turned legs and spindles is time consuming.

3 Bentwood chairs
A hot-caustic dip may distort bentwood furniture. If you don't want to remove the finish by hand, have these items stripped in a cold-chemical or warm-alkali dip.

4 Carved woodwork
Industrial stripping is safe for most solid-wood items, but sanding raised grain from carved wood is a real chore. It may be better to strip these items yourself with a chemical paint or varnish remover (see pages 32–3).

5 Antique woodwork
It is always best to strip antiques by hand. This allows you the option of removing just some of the finish to undertake a repair (see page 34).

6 Veneered pieces
Hot caustic soda can lift veneers off the groundwork. It would be unwise to use any industrial process unless the company concerned is prepared to guarantee their safety.

CHEMICAL STRIPPERS

Perhaps the most efficient method of removing finishes from any item of woodwork, be it a fine piece of furniture or an old pine door, is to apply a chemical stripper that partially dissolves the varnish, paint or polish, making a thick sludge that you can scrape and wash from the surface. You can strip wax polish with white spirit, and small areas of French polish using methylated spirit (see page 34), but commercially prepared paint and varnish removers are far more potent and will enable you to strip any finish, even if you cannot identify it precisely.

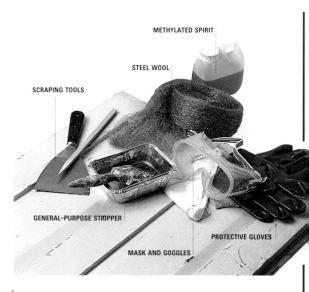

METHYLATED SPIRIT

STEEL WOOL

SCRAPING TOOLS

GENERAL-PURPOSE STRIPPER

PROTECTIVE GLOVES

MASK AND GOGGLES

Commercial paint and varnish removers
An extensive range of products is available, so you should be able to find a stripper that will suit your requirements. Most types of finish remover are available from any hardware store that stocks paints and varnishes.

General-purpose strippers
These are the most commonly available strippers, form-ulated to remove any finish, including water-based paints and varnishes. They are generally fairly corrosive substances and should be handled with care. Since some of them also exude unpleasant fumes, it pays to wear a face mask when using them.

Varnish removers
Since a few modern finishes are resistant to general-purpose strippers, some manufacturers also market special strippers that will soften the toughest varnish. They may be even more potent than general-purpose strippers, so follow the maker's handling instructions with care.

Safe strippers
So-called safe strippers, the latest generation of finish removers, do not release harmful fumes and can generally be handled without wearing protective gloves. Allow extra time when working with safe strippers, as the chemicals react relatively slowly with certain finishes.

Liquid and gel strippers
Many finish removers are available in two consistencies, to suit the nature of the workpiece. Thick gel-like strippers cling to any vertical or horizontal surface, and are therefore the best choice for built-in furniture or any workpiece that cannot be laid flat on a bench. A liquid version of the stripper is better able to cope with delicate carving and mouldings, but is more difficult to control.

Spirit- or water-washable
Having removed the softened finish, it is necessary to wash the workpiece to remove all traces of stripper. Water is often recommended by the manufacturer, and is a good choice to avoid an excess of solvent fumes in the workshop. However, to protect marquetry and other delicate veneers from the effects of water, choose a stripper that can be washed off with white spirit.

SAFETY PRECAUTIONS
Using chemical strippers is not dangerous, provided you follow sensible precautions and always comply with the printed instructions supplied with each particular stripper.

- Work outdoors or in a well-ventilated workshop.
- Wear a face mask or respirator to protect yourself from harmful fumes.
- Wear protective gloves, goggles and old clothes when handling corrosive strippers.
- Cover the workbench and floor with sheets of polythene or newspaper.
- Check with your local authority on how best to dispose of hazardous waste materials.

Using chemical strippers

Unless a manufacturer suggests other methods for using a particular chemical stripper, you can assume the following procedures apply to any type of paint or varnish remover. Prepare the workshop, pour some stripper into a shallow dish, and select an old paintbrush to apply it.

1 Applying the stripper

Brush a liberal coat of finish remover onto the workpiece, stippling it into carving and mouldings. Some varnishes and paints might be slow to react, but eventually the surface will begin to wrinkle.

After 10 to 15 minutes, check that the finish has softened right through to the wood by scraping a small area. If the lower coats of finish are still intact, apply fresh stripper, stippling the partly softened layers back down again.

2 Scraping off the surface

Leave the stripper to penetrate for another few minutes, then scrape the softened finish from the wood with a wide-blade paint scraper and wipe it onto a thick wad of newspaper. Fold the newspaper to wrap the waste and place it outside to dry, ready for disposal.

3 Cleaning irregular surfaces

Use a shavehook to scrape finish from mouldings, then rub along them with fine steel wool to clean out the residue, turning the pad inside out as it becomes clogged. Use an abrasive nylon pad on oak and to wipe softened paint or varnish from turned legs and spindles. Sharpen a short length of dowel to pick solvent and paint from deep carving and tight corners.

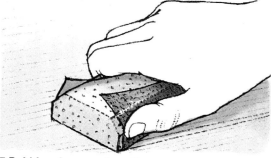

4 Washing the workpiece

Clean every speck of finish out of the grain by rubbing the wood with balls of steel wool or a nylon pad dipped in fresh stripper. Wash the workpiece thoroughly with water or white spirit, and leave it to dry.

5 Rubbing down and sealing

Sand the wood lightly to remove raised grain (see page 19) and, unless you know the history of the workpiece, apply a sanding sealer (see page 26) to make sure there is no chance of silicone oil contaminating the new finish. If you are afraid sanding sealer might affect the clarity of the finish, seal the wood with a coat of transparent shellac polish.

Stripping small areas

If you need to expose just a small area of wood, perhaps to bleach out a dark stain (see page 30), there is no need to strip the entire piece. To make the job of matching the original finish as easy as possible, strip an area with definable edges, a table top, for example, a drawer front or side panel. Set up the piece so that the area you intend to strip is horizontal, and use a gel-consistency stripper for better control.

If you can identify the finish (see page 28), you may be able to use its solvent to soften and remove it. Being relatively gentle, straightforward solvents enable you to feather the edge of a stripped patch, keeping the area to a bare minimum. However, colour matching the finish is likely to be more critical and the liquid nature of solvents makes them difficult to control.

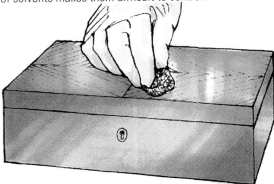

Removing French polish

Pour some methylated spirit into a shallow dish and dip a small ball of fine steel wool into it. Gently rub away at the finish until it begins to soften, then wipe it off with a cloth pad.

If there is a risk of meths running onto adjacent areas of polish, dampen a cloth pad with meths and use it to wet the surface, then abrade the polish gently with dry steel wool or an abrasive nylon pad.

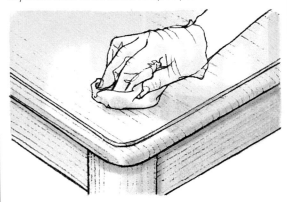

Stripping wax polish

You can use a similar process to remove a patch of wax polish from a workpiece, using white spirit.

INDUSTRIAL STRIPPING

To save time and effort, consider having large items stripped professionally. Industrial stripping tanks accommodate most items of furniture and joinery, and many companies will collect them from your house and deliver them after stripping.

Hot caustic dip

The most economical process involves immersing workpieces in hot caustic soda, followed by a thorough hosing with water to wash the chemical out of the wood. This is a most efficient system for removing finishes, but consider carefully the risks involved before you submit old furniture to what, after all, is fairly harsh treatment for items made from wood. Exposure to heat and water causes the wood to expand and contract considerably, often leading to weak joints, warped components and split panels. At the very least, you can expect raised grain and perhaps some staining. Since the same conditions soften animal glues, veneered pieces may blister or even delaminate.

Cold-chemical dip

Some companies operate with a cold-chemical solution that is less harmful for solid-wood items, but is relatively expensive compared with caustic soda. You must expect a certain amount of raised grain, and it would be unwise to have veneered items stripped unless the company will guarantee their safety.

Warm-alkali dip

You can have pieces dipped for a few minutes only in a warm-alkali solution. This is a carefully controlled process that is safe for all man-made boards, including plywood, but you should still ask for advice before having old veneered furniture stripped.

HOT-AIR STRIPPERS

You can strip oil-based finishes by heating them until they are soft enough to be scraped from the wood. Using a traditional gas torch is a little risky because, until you get used to handling the tool, it is fairly easy to scorch the wood. However, after a little practice, anyone can use an electric hot-air stripper to remove paint from larger items of built-in furniture and joinery. Being lightweight, a modern stripper, which can be fitted with various nozzles to direct the heat, is easy to control and use for long periods.

1 Softening the finish
Holding the nozzle of the stripper about 50mm (2in) from the surface of the workpiece, squeeze the trigger and move the tool slowly from side to side until the paint begins to blister and lift off the wood.

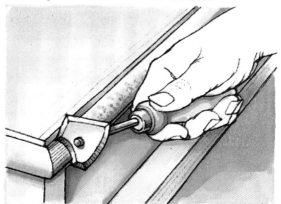

2 Scraping off softened paint
As soon as the finish softens, switch off the stripper and lift the paint from the wood, using a decorator's scraper. Use a shavehook to scrape softened paint from mouldings, taking care not to gouge the wood with the blade points.

3 Cleaning the surface
It may prove impossible to scrape every speck of paint from the pores of an open-grain timber. This doesn't matter if you plan to repaint the piece; simply fill any blemishes, sand the wood lightly and apply a primer. If you want to apply a clear finish, clean out the grain with steel wool or an abrasive nylon pad dipped in chemical paint stripper, then wash and seal the wood (see page 33).

MECHANICAL STRIPPING
Because you have to sand the wood in any case, removing a finish with a power sander would appear to be a viable option. However, it is practically impossible to avoid sanding away some of the wood, the dust created is particularly hazardous, and all but fairly coarse abrasives clog almost immediately. In addition, you still have to sand anything but flat surfaces by hand.

A cabinet scraper creates less dust and is more controllable, but even so scraping a finish from a large item would be somewhat laborious. A scraper comes into its own when you need to remove just a small patch of finish to repair the wood beneath, especially if there are adjacent areas that you want to protect from moisture, heat, or chemical strippers.

DEALING WITH INFESTATION

The common furniture beetle, better known as woodworm, can inhabit any form of woodwork, and the thriving market in used furniture means that a wormed piece can crop up just about anywhere. There is no point in refinishing old furniture that is infested with wood-boring insects until they have been eradicated.

The damage is the result of the insect larvae burrowing deeply into the wood for a period of three to four years. However, the first signs of infestation are usually a few round flight holes in the surface of the wood where the adult beetles emerged, prior to laying their eggs elsewhere.

Checking the extent of infestation
Most outbreaks of woodworm are treatable, provided the wood is still structurally sound. Use the point of a knife blade to probe the wood in the vicinity of obvious infestation; if the wood crumbles under pressure, that component will have to be repaired or even replaced. If the wood appears to be firm, treat it with a chemical preservative, formulated to kill any remaining larvae and prevent future infestation.

DETECTING WOODWORM
Although you may detect flight holes in polished surfaces, the beetle lays its eggs on unfinished wood, so always check those parts for signs of infestation. Take out the drawers, for example, and inspect them all round, including the bottom panels. Similarly check the backs of cabinets and the undersides of tables and sideboards. Pale-coloured flight holes and traces of fine wood dust indicate recent infestation.

A used piece of furniture that you have acquired may have been treated for woodworm already. However, if there is any doubt, it pays to treat the piece yourself.

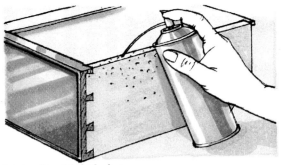

1 Injecting flight holes
The inside of infested wood is probably honeycombed with interconnecting tunnels. Inject a chemical preservative deep into the wood by squirting the fluid into a flight hole every 50mm (2in) or so. Fluid is supplied in cans with pointed nozzles for this purpose, or in aerosol cans fitted with narrow plastic hoses. Always protect your eyes, in case fluid shoots out from another flight hole under pressure.

2 Treating bare wood
Since it is impossible to know how far the larvae have burrowed, pour some fluid into a dish and paint it onto all unfinished surfaces. Preservative smells unpleasant so, if possible, work outside and wear a face mask. Leave the work to dry out, then treat it a second time. After the preservative has dried a second time, you can apply any finish to the wood.

3 Treating polished areas
There is no point in painting preservative onto polished surfaces, since it cannot penetrate the wood. As an extra precaution against future infestation, apply an insecticidal polish to old finished surfaces. Fill flight holes with coloured wax sticks (see page 11).

CHAPTER 3 The idea of artificially colouring a piece of wood may seem unnecessary when the various species of timber are so colourful already. However, stains are mostly applied to enhance the natural colour of a particular workpiece, or perhaps to unify several similar pieces of wood that vary slightly in their hue or tone.

COLOURING WOOD

BLEACHING WOOD

Woodworkers often resort to bleaching in order to obliterate staining. For this, you should use a comparatively mild bleach, such as a solution of oxalic acid (see page 30). However, it may also be desirable to reduce the depth of colour of a workpiece, perhaps so that you can stain it to resemble a different species, or maybe to stain several components the same colour. To alter the colour of timbers drastically, you need a strong proprietary two-part bleach. This is usually sold in kit form, comprising a pair of clearly labelled plastic bottles, one containing an alkali and the other hydrogen peroxide. However, the bottles are invariably labelled A and B, or 1 and 2.

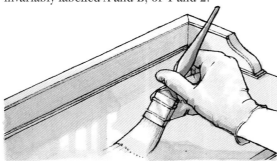

1 Applying solution A
Pour some of the contents of bottle A into a glass or plastic container and, using a white-fibre or nylon brush, wet the workpiece evenly. Don't splash bleach onto adjacent surfaces and, if you have to work on a vertical surface, start at the bottom to avoid runs streaking the surface.

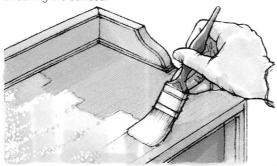

2 Applying solution B
About 5 to 10 minutes later, during which time the wood may darken, take another brush and apply the second solution. The chemical reaction causes foaming on the surface of the wood.

Testing the effectiveness of bleach
Because some woods bleach better than others, it is worth testing a sample before you treat the actual workpiece. As a rough guide, ash, beech, elm and sycamore are easy to bleach, whereas you may have to bleach other woods, such as mahogany, rosewood, oak and padauk, a second time to get the colour you want.

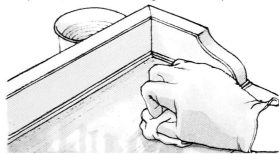

3 Neutralizing the bleach
When it is dry, or as soon as the wood is the required colour, neutralize the bleach by washing the work with a weak acetic-acid solution, comprising one teaspoon of white vinegar in a pint of water. Put the work aside for about three days, then sand down the raised grain and apply the finish.

SAFETY PRECAUTIONS
Wood bleach is a dangerous substance which must be handled with care and stored in the dark, out of the reach of children.

• Wear protective gloves, goggles and an apron.

• Wear a face mask when sanding wood that has been bleached.

• Ventilate the workshop or work outside.

• Have a supply of water handy so that you can rinse your skin immediately if you splash yourself with bleach. If you are going to work outside, fill a bucket with water.

• If you get bleach in your eyes, rinse well with running water and seek medical attention.

• Never mix the two solutions except on the wood, and always apply them with separate brushes. Discard any unused bleach.

LIMING WOOD

Strictly speaking, liming does not actually change the colour of the wood, but because its open pores are filled with a special white wax, the appearance of the wood alters dramatically. Liming wax, a proprietary blend of waxes and pigments, is available from most wood-finish suppliers.

Prepare the workpiece, sanding it smooth, then wipe the surface with a cloth dampened with white spirit to remove traces of grease.

Liming wax accentuates large open pores

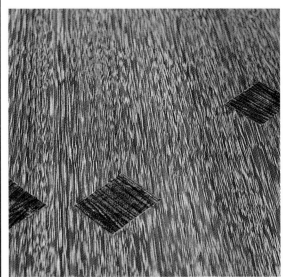

1 Opening the grain
Using a bronze-wire brush, scrub the wood in the direction of the grain to clean out the pores. Glance across the work from time to time to check your progress, ensuring that you cover the surface evenly. Wipe the debris from the surface with a tack rag.

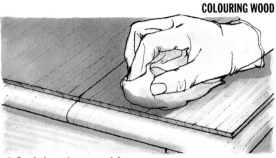

2 Staining the wood for contrast
Because the effect of liming depends on the contrast between the wax and the colour of the wood, it often pays to stain the work first. Use a water stain and seal in the colour with a coat of transparent shellac polish (see page 53). When the sealer coat is dry, smooth the surface with an abrasive nylon pad.

3 Applying liming wax
Dip a pad of burlap into liming wax and apply it to the work, using firm circular strokes to force it into the pores. When you have covered the surface, wipe across the grain to remove excess wax. After 10 minutes or so, gently burnish the surface in the direction of the grain, using a soft cloth pad.

4 Finishing the work
Leave the liming wax to harden for 24 hours, then apply an ordinary paste wax polish (see page 91) to enhance the colour of the wood.

Liming wax prevents varnish or cold-cure lacquer setting properly. If you want to apply one of these finishes, follow the procedure described above, but use white decorator's undercoat instead of liming wax. Having rubbed paint into the pores, wipe it from the surface, using a paper towel slightly dampened with white spirit.

CHEMICAL STAINING

It was once common practice to colour oak and other woods that are rich in tannic acid by exposing them to ammonia fumes. Depending on the length of exposure, fuming will cause a piece of oak to turn anything from a pale honey colour to a fairly dark golden brown. The colour is even and permanent, yet does not obscure the grain pattern. You might decide to fume new components before assembling them or, depending on its size, fume the completed workpiece.

Fume the wood before filling blemishes, as wood putties and fillers are not affected by ammonia fumes. Even more importantly, any steel that is in contact with the wood causes black stains, so make sure that no screw heads are exposed, and avoid fitting metal hardware until after fuming.

Fumed and limed European-oak cabinet (top)

Detail of cabinet constructed from strips of fumed and natural oak (above)

Sycamore shelf unit with fumed-oak drawer cabinet (left)

Obtaining ammonia

You can fume wood using ordinary household ammonia, but the process will be relatively slow. For faster results use 26 per cent ammonia, also known as '880' or 'eight-eighty', which you can buy from a pharmacist. For safety, wear protective gloves and a respirator when handling this strong ammonia solution and, if possible, work outside.

Making and using a fume tent

To concentrate the ammonia fumes, enclose the workpiece inside a makeshift timber framework, draped with black plastic sheeting. If you are fuming separate components, support them face-side up on wooden wedges or pyramids to keep the points of contact to a minimum. Place shallow dishes of ammonia inside the fume tent, then make it airtight by sealing all joints with adhesive tape. Oak will turn a medium-dark colour after about 24 hours of exposure, but check on progress from time to time, and remove the work when it is just slightly lighter than required – the wood continues to change colour for a while after you take it out of the tent.

EBONIZING

The tannic-acid content of wood can also be used to turn it black, a process known as ebonizing. Traditionally, ebonizing was carried out with vinegar in which pieces of iron had been left for several days.

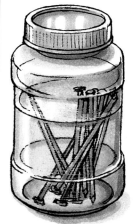

Ebonizing a workpiece

Leave a handful of rust-free steel nails in a jar of white vinegar for about a week, then paint it liberally and evenly onto the wood. Try diluting with water to achieve different tones. Let the wood dry, then brush on some ammonia to neutralize the acetic acid. Leave the work to dry again and apply a sealer.

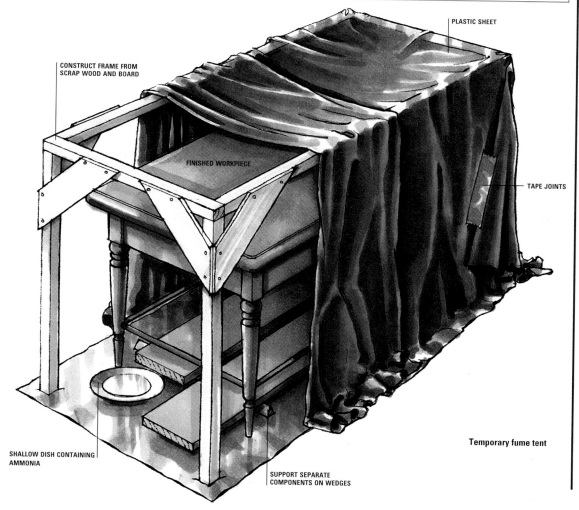

PLASTIC SHEET

CONSTRUCT FRAME FROM
SCRAP WOOD AND BOARD

FINISHED WORKPIECE

TAPE JOINTS

SHALLOW DISH CONTAINING
AMMONIA

SUPPORT SEPARATE
COMPONENTS ON WEDGES

Temporary fume tent

STAINING WOOD

A wood stain or dye is fundamentally different from a surface finish such as paint or varnish. Paint, which colours the wood by depositing a relatively dense layer of pigments on the surface, also forms a protective coating on the workpiece, and clear varnish is essentially a paint without the coloured pigments. A true penetrating dye or stain soaks into the wood, taking the colour deep into the fibres. However, it provides no protection at all, and so a clear finish is always applied to a stained workpiece afterwards.

Modern stains often contain translucent pigments that lodge in the pores of the wood, accentuating the grain. However, without thorough testing, it can be difficult to determine which ready-made stains contain pigments because a manufacturer may create a whole range of stains, only some of which contain pigments to create particular colours. Successive applications of a pigmented stain gradually darken the wood, whereas applying more than one coat of a non-pigmented stain has little effect on the colour.

1 Solvent or oil stains
2 Acrylic stains
3 Methylated spirit
4 Ready-mixed water stains
5 White spirit
6 Ready-mixed spirit stains
7 Concentrated water stains
8 Powdered water stains

Solvent or oil stains

The most widely available penetrating stains, made from oil-soluble dyes, are thinned with white spirit. Known as solvent stains or oil stains, these wood dyes are easy to apply evenly, will not raise the grain and dry relatively quickly. Oil stains are made in a wide range of wood-like colours, which you can mix to achieve intermediate shades. Some solvent stains contain translucent pigments that make them fade-resistant.

Spirit stains

Traditional spirit stains are made by dissolving aniline dyes in methylated spirit. The main disadvantage with spirit stains is their extremely rapid drying time, which makes it difficult to get even coverage without leaving darker patches of overlapping colour. Some manufacturers supply ready-mixed stains, and they are also available in powder form which you can mix with meths and a little thinned shellac as a binder. Concentrated powder stains, which come in a limited range of strong colours, are used mainly for tinting French polish.

Water stains

Water stains are available from specialists as ready-made wood-colour dyes. You can also buy them as crystals or powders for dissolving in hot water so that you can mix any colour you want. Water stains dry slowly, which means there is plenty of time to achieve an even distribution of colour, but you must allow adequate time for the water to evaporate completely before you apply a finish. They also raise the grain, leaving a rough surface, so it is essential to wet the wood and sand down prior to applying water stains (see page 20).

Acrylic stains

The latest generation of water stains, based on acrylic resins, are emulsions that leave a film of colour on the surface of the wood. They raise the grain less than traditional water stains and are more resistant to fading. As well as the usual wood-like colours, acrylic stains are made in a range of pastel shades; it can, however, be difficult to predict the final colour produced by these pastel-coloured stains on dark hardwoods. All acrylic stains need diluting by about 10 per cent when used on dense hardwoods.

COMPATIBILITY

You can create practically any colour you like by mixing compatible wood stains or dyes, and you can reduce the strength of a colour by adding more of the relevant solvent. However, you should guard against overlaying a penetrating stain, even one that has dried out, with a surface finish that contains a similar solvent. As you drag a brush or pad across the surface, the solvent may reactivate the colour, causing it to 'bleed' into the surface finish.

As a basic rule, select a stain that will not react with the finish you want to apply, or seal the stain first to prevent solvent disturbing the colour. It is always worth testing the stain and finish before applying either to a workpiece.

Solvent stains

Seal a solvent stain (oil stain) with shellac or sanding sealer before applying a varnish, lacquer or wax polish that is thinned with white spirit, turpentine or cellulose thinner.

Spirit stains

You can use a spirit stain under any finish, except for French polish. When the stained surface is completely dry, gently wipe it with a clean rag before applying a finish.

Water and acrylic stains

Allow a stain thinned with water to dry for 48 hours before overlaying with a solvent-based finish – any moisture that has not evaporated can cause the finish to develop a white haze or milkiness. Although a dry water stain should not react with a water-based finish, always test the finish in an inconspicuous place before you apply it.

If you forget to raise the grain before applying a water stain (see page 20), rub down the stained surface very lightly with 220 grit abrasive paper, and then pick up the dust with a tack rag before applying any finish.

APPLYING PENETRATING STAINS

Wet the surface to get some idea of what a particular workpiece will look like under a clear finish, and if in doubt, apply some of the actual finish you intend to use. If you are unhappy with its depth of colour, or if you feel it doesn't quite match another piece of wood you are working with, take a scrap piece of the same timber and make a test strip to try out a stain before colouring the workpiece itself (see opposite).

Setting up for staining
Plan the work sequence in advance, to minimize the possibility of stain running onto adjacent surfaces or one area of colour drying before you can 'pick up' the wet edges. If you have to colour both sides of a workpiece, stain the least important side first, immediately wiping off any dye that runs over the edges.

Staining large panels
If possible, set up the workpiece so that the surface to be stained is horizontal. Lay a large panel or door on a pair of trestles so that you can approach it from all sides.

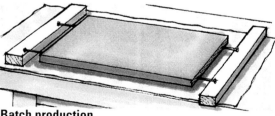

Batch production
It is sometimes convenient to stain components before assembly, setting them aside to dry while you complete the batch.

To colour a number of adjustable bookshelves, for example, drive a pair of nails or screws into each end. Lay each shelf on a bench, with the nails or screws resting on battens to raise the shelf off the work surface. Having stained each side in turn, stand the shelf on end against a wall until the stain is dry.

Applicators
You can use good-quality paintbrushes, decorators' paint pads covered with mohair pile, non-abrasive polishing pads (see page 17), or a wad of soft cloth to apply penetrating stains. You can also spray wood dyes, provided you have adequate extraction facilities (see page 83). Wear PVC gloves and old clothes or an apron when applying wood stains.

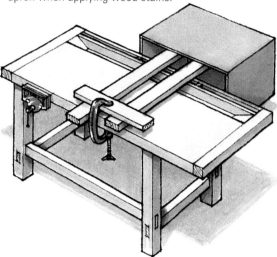

Supporting drawers and cabinets
After staining the inside of drawers or small cabinets, support them at a comfortable working height to complete the job, using cantilevered battens clamped or screwed temporarily to a bench.

Preparing a workpiece for staining
Sand the workpiece well (see pages 19–24), making sure there are no scratches or defects that will absorb more stain than the surrounding wood. In addition, scrape off any patches of dried glue that could affect the absorption of stain.

Staining a flat surface

Pour enough stain to colour the entire workpiece into a shallow dish. Brush or swab the stain onto the wood in the direction of the grain, blending in the wet edges before the dye has time to dry. When you have covered the surface, take a clean cloth pad, and mop up excess stain, distributing it evenly across the workpiece. If you splash stain onto the wood, blend it in quickly to prevent a patchy appearance.

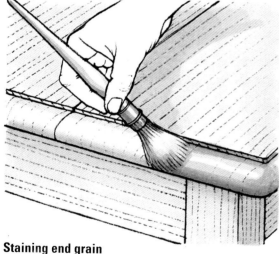

Staining end grain

Exposed end grain appears darker than the rest of the workpiece because the orientation of the cells allows it to absorb more penetrating stain. Painting the end grain with a coat of white shellac or sanding sealer will reduce the amount of colour taken up by the wood. Alternatively, you can use thinned varnish, but you should wait 24 hours before you stain the wood.

MAKING A TEST STRIP

Before you colour an actual workpiece, make a test strip to see how the wood will be affected by the stain you intend to use. It is important that the test strip is sanded as smooth as the workpiece you will be staining, because coarsely sanded wood absorbs more dye and will therefore appear darker than the same piece of wood prepared with a finer sandpaper.

Apply a coat of stain and allow it to dry. As a general rule, stains dry lighter than they appear when wet. Apply a second coat to see if it darkens the wood, leaving part of the first application exposed for comparison. If you apply more than two full coats of stain, the colour may become patchy due to uneven absorption of the liquid.

A second coat of a non-pigmented stain may not change the colour appreciably, but you can modify it by overlaying with a compatible stain of a different colour.

Once the stain is completely dry, paint one half of the test strip with the intended finish to see how it affects the colour of the stain.

Test strip, using pigmented stain

Test strip, using non-pigmented stain

Colouring veneer

You can treat modern veneered panels like solid wood. However, old furniture was invariably veneered using water-soluble animal glue, and it would pay to use a spirit or solvent stain to colour such items.

You can stain veneer patches (see page 15) or pieces of marquetry before gluing them in place. Dipping scraps of veneer in a dish of wood dye ensures even colouring.

Staining turned spindles

Apply stain to turned legs and spindles with a rag or a non-woven polishing pad. Rub the dye well into turned beads and fluting, then cup the applicator around the leg or spindle and rub it lengthways.

Since turned work exposes end grain it is very difficult to obtain even coverage.

Staining carved work

Use a soft brush to apply penetrating stain to carving or intricate mouldings, absorbing surplus stain immediately with rag or a paper towel.

STAINING SOFTWOOD

It is advisable to apply stain to softwood with a cloth pad rather than a paintbrush; highly absorbent wood tends to draw extra stain from a heavily loaded brush at the first point of contact, thus creating a patch of darker colour.

The different rates of absorption between early-wood and latewood often give stained softwood a distinctly striped appearance. With some colours, this can be very attractive, but if it doesn't suit your requirements, try colouring the wood with varnish stain or staining wax (see opposite).

Softwood coloured with penetrating stain (left) and varnish stain

STAINED FINISHES

Certain products enable you to modify the colour of wood and provide a protective finish at the same time. Stained finishes do not have the same clarity as a penetrating wood dye and, because they lie on the surface of the wood, applying too many coats tends to obscure the grain. Varnish stains and protective wood stains are brushed onto the wood. Apply staining wax like wax polish (see pages 92–3).

Staining waxes

There are numerous coloured wax polishes that can be used directly on bare wood, but they cannot match the depth of colour of a penetrating wood dye. Their primary value is in modifying the colour of a finished piece and blending in faded patches.

Coloured waxes look very much darker in the tin than they do on a workpiece. Even deep-brown polish, for example, will add a deep rich tint to pine without obliterating the grain.

Protective wood stains

Protective wood stains are translucent finishes for exterior joinery. Being water-vapour-permeable, they allow the wood to exude moisture while protecting it against adverse weather conditions. As a result, protective stains are long-lasting finishes that resist flaking and cracking.

The majority of protective wood stains are tinted, but there is also a clear variety for refurbishing previously stained wood without altering the colour. Protective wood stains are either water-based or solvent-based, and some are one-coat finishes. The water-based variety may not dry properly if applied during wet or humid weather.

Varnish stains

Varnish stains are basically tinted polyurethane or acrylic varnishes that contain colouring agents in the form of translucent pigments or oil-soluble dyes. They are ideal for putting colour back into a dowdy workpiece that is already varnished. Although stained varnishes are tough finishes, it pays to overlay them with clear varnish, to prevent scratches and heavy wear that will reveal the paler wood beneath the layer of colour. Varnish stains must be brushed on evenly to avoid a streaky appearance.

Exterior wood stain brings protection and colour to a softwood deck

MODIFYING THE COLOUR

No matter how practised you become at judging colours and mixing dyes, inevitably there comes a time when the dried stain is not quite the colour you had in mind. If it's too dark, you may be able to remove some stain, but don't make the mistake of trying to alter the colour by applying layer upon layer of dye – this will simply lead to muddy colours or poor finish adhesion. Instead, add washes of tinted finish to modify the colour gradually.

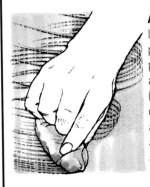

Adding tinted shellac
If the wood is to be French-polished, dissolve some powdered stain in meths and add it to a pale shellac (see page 58). Apply a coat of the tinted shellac and allow it to dry. Keep adding washes of shellac, adjusting the colour with spirit stain, until you achieve the right shade.

Applying tinted varnish
If you plan to varnish the workpiece, you can apply a sealer coat of tinted shellac. Alternatively, use a thinned wash of varnish stain, or add diluted wood dye to a compatible clear varnish. Gradually build up to the required tone with a series of thin coats, then apply a protective coat of full-strength varnish.

Toning with wax
If the colour match is still not perfect, you can finally tip the balance by adding a dressing of coloured staining wax. Rub on the wax in the direction of the grain, using an abrasive nylon pad or very fine steel wool, then buff it to a satin finish with a soft cloth.

Removing colour
If a solvent-stained workpiece dries streaky or too dark in tone, wet the surface with white spirit and rub it with an abrasive nylon pad. Wipe the surface with a cloth to lift some of the stain and redistribute the remainder more evenly. At this stage, you can modify the colour of the wood by applying another, paler stain while the wood is still damp.

ACCENTUATING MOULDINGS AND CARVING
You can bring a workpiece to life by using colour to add depth to carving and intricate mouldings. The process imitates the effects of natural wear, adding considerably to the appeal of antique or reproduction furniture and picture frames.

Highlighting
The simplest method is to wipe colour from the high points while the stain is wet. Alternatively, sand these areas lightly with an abrasive pad after the stain has dried, and wash off the dust, using a cloth dampened with solvent.

Shading
You can add depth to the most delicate of raised patterns, using dark stain mixed into diluted French polish (see left). Seal the stained surface, then paint tinted shellac liberally onto carved and moulded areas of the workpiece, allowing it to flow into all the nooks and crannies. Wipe the colour off high points immediately, using a soft cloth, and allow the shellac to dry before applying a clear finish.

CHAPTER 4

French-polishing is the traditional method of applying shellac dissolved in methylated spirit, using a soft cloth pad known as a rubber to apply the polish. It is an essential skill to master if you want to restore reasonably priced antique furniture, because during Victorian times it was as common a finish as polyurethane varnish is today.

FRENCH POLISH

SHELLAC PRODUCTION

Shellac, the basic ingredient for French polish, is derived from an insect, *Laciffer lacca*, a native of India and the far East. The larvae of the lac insect secrete a protective resin that builds up in thick layers on the twigs and branches of trees on which they feed. The spread of the insect is encouraged by tying infested shoots to other suitable host trees. Eventually, when twigs become encrusted with hardened lac resin, they are 'harvested' as stick lac for refining into a wide variety of products, including shellac polish.

Handmade shellac

Although the production of shellac has been largely mechanized, traditional methods that have been practised for hundreds of years still account for approximately 15 per cent of the world's shellac.

The crop of encrusted twigs is pounded and scraped to remove the lac resin, which is then crushed and sieved to extract wood fragments and insect remains. The crushed resin is washed in water, then rinsed and spread out in the sun to dry. After drying, it is sieved again and winnowed to produce a commercial grade of resin known as seed lac.

Blended seed lac is packed into a narrow canvas tube which is suspended in front of a charcoal fire. As the resin melts, the tube is twisted, wringing molten shellac through the weave of the canvas. The shellac is transferred to a cylindrical ceramic jar filled with hot water, where it is smoothed out to an even thickness. Peeling the sheet of soft shellac from the cylinder, a skilled worker stretches it in front of the fire, using his hands, feet, and even his teeth. Once it is removed from the heat, the shellac cools rapidly and is crushed to make flake shellac.

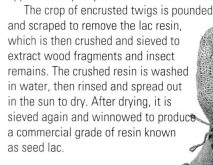

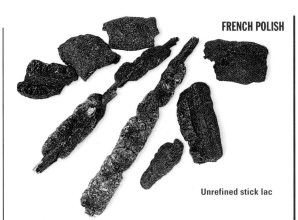

Unrefined stick lac

A different variety of handmade shellac is made by dropping the molten lac onto cold stone or sheets of galvanized iron, where it solidifies into flat discs, 50 to 75mm (2 to 3in) in diameter. These translucent discs, which can be inspected against the light for possible impurities, are reserved for the best-quality button polish. Button lac is also produced by pouring the molten shellac into moulds.

Stretching shellac which will be crushed into flakes when cool

Modern production methods

Though traditional methods are still employed at village level, modern manufacturing processes are geared to producing flake shellac in various qualities and colours.

Seed lac is heated with steam until it becomes molten enough to be filtered in hydraulic presses, and then is passed through rollers which produce long continuous sheets of shellac.

Alternatively, seed lac is dissolved in industrial alcohol, and the solution is filtered to remove impurities. The alcohol is boiled off to leave molten shellac which is passed through rollers.

1 Machine-made flakes
Modern manufacturing processes produce very fine flake shellac.

2 Handmade flakes
Traditional handmade flakes are relatively thick.

3 Stick lac
Coarse lac resin scraped from twigs and branches.

4 Seed lac
Crushed and processed stick lac becomes commercial seed lac.

5 Button lac
Translucent discs of best-quality shellac.

6 Blond shellac flakes
De-waxed flakes for making your own almost-clear French polish (see page 53).

7 Bleached shellac
Bleached de-waxed shellac for manufacturing commercial transparent polish (see page 53).

KNOTTING AND SANDING SEALERS

As well as being the basic ingredient for French polish, shellac is also useful as a sealer, forming an effective barrier that prevents contaminants affecting a surface finish. An application of French polish or shellac-based sanding sealer, for example, prevents wood stain migrating into a top coat of varnish (see page 26). Shellac is also used to manufacture fast-drying knotting which, when painted over knots and end grain, seals in softwood resins that might otherwise stain paint or varnish. If you plan to use a catalysed lacquer, however, use only de-waxed shellac as a sealer.

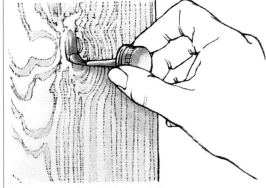

Apply two coats of knotting before priming

READY-MADE POLISHES

It is possible to buy flake shellac from which you can make your own polish but, unless cost is of prime importance, it is invariably more convenient to use one of the many varieties of commercially prepared shellac polishes.

Standard polish

The basic medium-brown French polish is manufactured from orange shellac flakes. It is suitable for polishing all dark hardwoods and for tinting pale-coloured species. Standard polish is widely available from most outlets, including hardware and paint suppliers.

French polish, prized for its glass-like finish, is ideal for elegant period-style furniture

White polish

Bleached seed lac is used to make a milky-white variety of polish, ideal for finishing pale-coloured hardwoods and for sealing wood prior to waxing. If standard white polish is too soft, you can buy one with additives that create a harder finish. White polish may not set properly after it has been in stock for about two years.

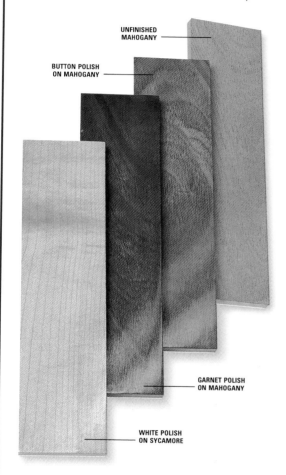

UNFINISHED MAHOGANY

BUTTON POLISH ON MAHOGANY

GARNET POLISH ON MAHOGANY

WHITE POLISH ON SYCAMORE

Pound cut

The 'strength' or viscosity of French polish is designated by how much shellac is dissolved in one gallon of alcohol, and is referred to as the 'cut', particularly in the USA. This specification is used even when polish is sold in litres. A ready-to-use 3 pound cut, for example, comprises about 30 per cent shellac, making it suitable for most general applications. A thinner, 1 pound cut would be more suitable as a sealer coat; in practice, however, most polishers would simply dilute the thicker 3 pound cut with alcohol.

Transparent polish

Shellac contains a small amount of wax which is insoluble in alcohol. It is this wax that accounts for the milkiness of white polish, and which settles out of other shellacs when they are left undisturbed for a period of time. Washing bleached shellac in petroleum solvent dissolves the wax, resulting in an almost clear polish that does not alter the natural colour of wood. Like white polish, transparent polish has a shelf life of about two years.

Button polish

The term button polish generally implies a superior-quality, golden-brown shellac polish. Although most ready-made polishes are made from good-quality flake shellac, some manufacturers still import traditional hand-made button lac for their polish.

De-waxed button polish is referred to as 'special' or 'transparent' button polish, and produces a harder finish than the standard variety.

Garnet polish

This is a deep red-brown French polish, popular with antique restorers. It is sometimes used to impart a reddish colour to mahogany and other similar woods.

Ebony polish

Black-stained ebony polish provides the typical glossy French-polish lustre, but obscures the grain if too much is applied. Ebony polish is the traditional piano finish, but is also used for polishing very dark woods.

Exterior French polishes

Exposure to water leaves white staining on all French polishes, except for a range of special dark and pale polishes that are specifically formulated for use on exterior woodwork.

BLONDE SHELLAC

Bleaching seed lac alters its properties, so that it becomes insoluble in alcohol after about three days. Because of its short shelf life, bleached shellac is only sold as ready-mixed polish (see above left). For wood finishers who prefer to make their own almost clear French polish, de-waxed blonde shellac flakes are available for dissolving in methylated spirit.

TRADITIONAL FRENCH-POLISHING

It is hard to imagine how French-polishing could have acquired a reputation for being so difficult to master when nineteenth-century polishers would have thought themselves unworthy of the title if they were unable to conjure up the perfect shellac finish. Now that we have become used to fast-drying varnishes and one-coat finishes, we seem to have lost the confidence to tackle a technique that requires time and patience to perfect. To become skilled at every aspect of French-polishing would take years of experience but, by practising basic techniques on pieces of scrap wood or veneered boards, any reasonably competent woodworker should be able to produce an acceptable result.

Although the Victorians French-polished practically every type of furniture imaginable, shellac is not particularly hard-wearing. It may be the perfect finish for a delicate side table, a sewing box, or even the best sideboard, but it would not be the ideal choice for a kitchen table or worktop, where it would be subjected to harsh treatment and regularly exposed to water, alcohol and heat (see page 30).

The type of wood you are using also affects whether to use shellac. French polish is at its best when applied to beautifully figured, close-grain hardwoods, such as mahogany, satinwood or walnut, but it seems inappropriate for open-grain oak or ash and the more mundane softwoods.

Creating a suitable environment
A clean, dust-free environment is necessary, whatever finish you are applying, but French polish is especially vulnerable to changes in temperature and humidity. Keep your workshop warm and dry, and draughtproof windows and doors.

If possible, set up your workbench in front of the main source of natural or artificial light so that it falls across the surface of the workpiece – you will be able to see how the polish is going on and detect foreign bodies or specks of dust immediately.

Making a rubber
Generations of polishers have refined and developed the techniques of French-polishing to suit individual tastes and requirements, but the essential elements remain the same – shellac is applied patiently over a period of days, gradually building a translucent film, using a rubber made by wrapping cotton wool in cloth.

Make the rubber to suit the size of your hand and surface area you will be polishing. The dimensions given in the following sequence are for a general-purpose rubber, but you may want to make smaller ones for specialized work.

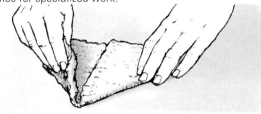

1 Folding the square of wadding
Upholsterer's wadding is the ideal material for a French-polishing rubber. Tear off a 150 to 225mm (6 to 9in) square of wadding, fold it in half, then fold over each half of the rectangle to make a triangle.

2 Shaping the wadding
Fold two corners of the triangle towards the centre, making a roughly sausage-shaped pad. If you are unable to obtain upholsterer's wadding, take a handful of ordinary unmedicated cotton wool and squeeze it into an egg-shape pad.

3 Inserting the wadding
Place the wadding diagonally across the centre of a 225 to 300mm (9 to 12in) square of soft cotton or linen. A piece of fabric torn from an old sheet or pillowcase is ideal, or you could use a large plain handkerchief.

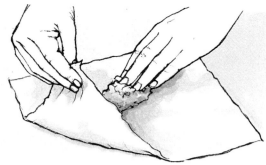

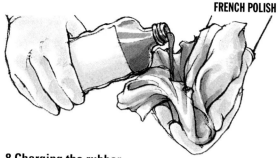

4 Folding over the covering

Taking hold of the corner, fold one half of the fabric over the end of the wadding pad.

5 Wrapping the wadding

Holding the wadding down with one hand, wrap the remaining corners over the pad to make a neat package.

6 Twisting excess fabric

Twist the fabric into a tail behind the pad to tighten up the package, then fold the tail over onto the pad to form a grip that fits in the palm of your hand.

7 Holding the rubber

Hold the rubber in one hand so that you can pinch the sides between forefinger and thumb, forming a pointed end with which to apply polish into tight corners. Make sure there are no creases or stitched hems running across the sole of the rubber.

8 Charging the rubber

You should never dip a rubber into polish, nor pour polish directly onto its sole. Instead, place the rubber in the palm of one hand and carefully unwrap it. Pour shellac polish onto the wadding, squeezing it gently until it is thoroughly wet but not completely saturated.

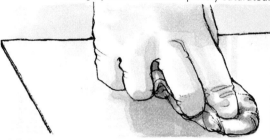

9 Stimulating the flow of polish

Re-wrap the rubber and press the sole against a flat surface to encourage the shellac to permeate the fabric, squeezing out excess polish that would build up in ridges on the workpiece. Use a piece of scrap wood or cardboard, or even the front rail of your bench, but make sure it is clean and free from dust. It will be necessary to recharge the rubber from time to time as the polish is used up.

STORING A RUBBER

To keep your rubber soft and supple between applications, store it in an airtight jar. A rubber may last for months, but discard it as soon as a hole wears in the fabric, before it begins to scar the polish. Even then, the used wadding without its cloth wrapping is useful as a 'fad' for sealing a workpiece with French polish (see page 56).

APPLYING FRENCH POLISH

Traditional polishing is a process that cannot be rushed. Any attempt to push on before applications of polish have been allowed to dry and harden inevitably leads to problems that retard progress rather than accelerate it.

French-polishing comprises three main stages. The wood must first be sealed as a prelude to the all-important 'bodying up', the process of building a satisfactory film of polish; this may take several days to complete. Finally, burnishing with meths removes excess oil and gives shellac its unique glossy finish. Although not absolutely essential, it pays to wear disposable gloves while polishing, to keep your hands clean.

1 Preparing the surface

Like most translucent finishes, French polish will accentuate the slightest flaw on the surface of the wood, so prepare the workpiece thoroughly. Repair any obvious blemishes, then sand the wood smooth (see pages 9–25). If necessary, colour the wood with stain (see pages 42–46) and apply a grain filler (see page 26). Alternatively, fill open grain by applying successive coats of polish, rubbing down with silicon-carbide paper between coats, until the pores are filled flush with shellac.

2 Sealing the wood

Professional polishers often use a 'fad' – a piece of used cotton wadding – to apply the first sealer coats of shellac polish, but a newly made rubber charged with slightly thinned polish works just as well. Apply the polish in long, overlapping strokes, parallel to the grain of the wood. In the early stages, you need apply very little pressure to the rubber; but as the work progresses, squeeze the rubber lightly to encourage more polish to flow. Don't go back over the work, even if you notice slight blemishes. When you have covered the entire work surface, leave the polish to harden for about an hour.

3 Rubbing down the sealer coat

Lightly sand the polished surface with fine silicon-carbide paper, in the direction of the grain only. If the first sealer coat is very uneven, apply another similar coat of polish.

4 Bodying up

Charge the rubber with full-strength polish, then begin building up the body of polish. The key to this stage is to keep the rubber moving while it is in contact with the work, preventing the sole sticking to the polish. Sweep the rubber onto the surface, making small, overlapping, circular strokes until you have coated the workpiece, then sweep the rubber off again.

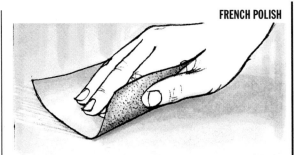

5 Polishing into corners

Make sure you polish right into closed or internal corners every time you coat a surface with French polish. This is where the pointed end of the rubber comes into play. Place your forefinger on top, then sweep the rubber into and out of the corner with one continuous movement.

6 Lubricating the rubber

As the work progresses, you will notice the rubber does not slide quite so easily across the surface; this is caused by the meths re-dissolving polish that has already begun to harden. Lubricate the rubber as soon as it begins to 'drag' by smearing a drop of linseed oil onto the sole with your fingertip.

7 Combining different strokes

To distribute the polish evenly, go back over the surface again, this time with figure-of-eight strokes, making sure you work right up to the edges. Finally, apply the polish with straight overlapping strokes, parallel to the grain. Leave the polish to dry for about 30 minutes, then repeat the whole process, perhaps three or four times. Put the workpiece aside to allow the polish to harden overnight.

8 Rubbing down

The next day, inspect the workpiece for specks of embedded dust or other blemishes and, if necessary, sand the surface very lightly, using self-lubricating silicon-carbide paper.

9 Building a protective body of polish

Continue to build up a thickness of polish, coating the surface three to four times per day, with a half-hour break between each coat, then allow the polish to harden overnight. Repeat the process over a period of days until you are satisfied with the general colour and appearance of the work.

10 Removing the oil

Lubricating the sole of the rubber leaves the polished surface streaky. To remove the oil from the polish and bring the surface to a gloss finish, add a little meths to the pad and squeeze it almost dry. Sweep the rubber across the work with straight parallel strokes, gradually increasing pressure until the rubber begins to drag, then leave the polish to harden. Repeat the process every two to three minutes until streaking disappears. Wrapping the pad with fresh fabric may help absorb the oil. After half an hour, polish the surface with a duster, then put the work aside for about a week to let the polish harden thoroughly.

Burnishing to a high gloss

If a polished surface does not shine to your satisfaction, you can burnish it after the shellac has hardened for a week. Rub the surface vigorously with a soft cloth moistened with a special-purpose burnishing cream or car-paint cleaner (see page 28). Both are extremely fine abrasives that will produce a deep shine. Finally, buff the polish with a dry duster.

Creating a satin finish

If a high gloss is not to your taste, you can cut back a newly French-polished workpiece, using a pad of 000-grade steel wool dipped in wax polish. Rub the hardened polish very lightly with the grain, until the entire surface appears to be matted evenly. Burnish gently with a duster.

Polishing carving and mouldings

It is impracticable to French-polish a deeply carved workpiece, or one with intricate mouldings, using a rubber. Instead, apply slightly diluted shellac polish with a soft squirrel-hair brush. Let the polish flow smoothly, but not too thickly, leaving it to settle naturally; over-brushing shellac leaves brushmarks in hardened polish.

Once the polish has hardened, burnish the high points, using a rubber moistened with meths (see page 57), but don't rub too hard. Polish with a duster.

ADJUSTING THE COLOUR

Perhaps the pinnacle of the French-polisher's art is the ability to modify the colour of the finish as the job progresses, a skill that requires great subtlety and which can only be learnt from experience.

There may be any number of reasons why modification might be necessary. If you are restoring old furniture, you may need to enrich a partly faded finish, for example, or perhaps you will want to adjust the shade of a component that does not quite match the colour of a new piece you are polishing.

As you build up the layers of polish, stand back from the work from time to time, and inspect it from all angles and in different lights to make sure it is progressing to your satisfaction.

Colouring shellac polish

A shift in colour is achieved by applying a wash coat or two of tinted shellac polish. These coats can be included at any time during the French-polishing process, then sealed and protected with subsequent layers of full-strength polish.

You can mix ready-made spirit stains with shellac, but professionals use powdered aniline dyes to tint French polish. They are available from specialist suppliers in a limited range of colours, typically red, black, yellow, green, blue, orange, and brown. The right combination of these colours will achieve any wood shade you require.

The secret is to mix very pale colours, so that you can overlay one with another to achieve the exact shade and tone required. Powdered dyes are very strong, so dissolve tiny amounts in meths and mix the solution in equal proportions with shellac polish.

Applying wash coats

After testing the coloured polish for strength on a piece of paper or scrap wood, apply it very thinly to the work with a fad or rubber. Try to blend it in, making sure there are no obvious edges to the coloured area. If using a rubber is impracticable, float it onto the work with a soft brush.

Let the polish dry, check it for accuracy and, if necessary, apply another wash coat to alter the balance of colour. If the edges of the tinted area are obvious, try sanding them lightly with a fine silicon-carbide paper.

Once you are satisfied with the result, continue bodying up the polish, using a rubber. Apply the first coats very gently to ensure you do not disturb or alter the colour.

BRUSHING SHELLAC

The idea of applying shellac by brush is not new. In the past, tradespeople such as coffin makers, whose work would probably not be viewed over-critically, tended to build up a body of polish by painting thinned shellac onto the wood. The traditional hand-rubbed appearance could always be achieved by finishing the job with a rubber.

If you have neither the inclination nor the time to learn true French-polishing, try one of the special brushing shellac polishes which contain additives to retard drying, enabling you to paint the shellac onto a workpiece without leaving permanent brushmarks in the finish. Use a soft, natural-bristle paintbrush.

Prepare and colour the work as recommended for traditional French-polishing.

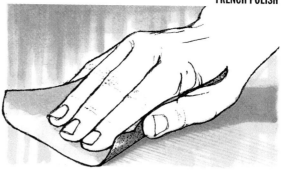

2 Rubbing down
Some brushing polishes dry faster than others, but an hour should be plenty of time. Using fine silicon-carbide paper, rub down the first coat lightly until it feels smooth, then apply two more coats of shellac. There's no need to rub down the second coat unless you notice any blemishes.

3 Waxing the finish
The result may be perfect for your needs straight from the brush, but you can modify the finish, to render it indistinguishable from a similar French-polished job, by rubbing it with fine steel wool dipped in wax polish. Apply the polish gently and evenly, making sure you don't cut through the layer of shellac.

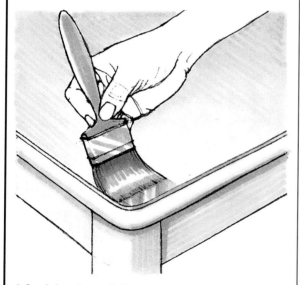

1 Applying the polish
Don't attempt to spread the finish as if it were varnish, but let the polish flow naturally from the brush, using straight strokes parallel with the grain. You can pick up runs or ridges of polish, provided you do it reasonably quickly. Flexing the bristles against the edges of the work tends to promote runs, so wipe them with a clean rag before the polish has time to set. If you notice too late, leave the runs to set, then rub them down later.

4 Buffing up the wax
Leave the wax to harden for 15 to 20 minutes, then burnish vigorously with a soft duster.

FAULTS AND REMEDIES

The following is a check list of common problems and solutions associated with French-polishing.

Pitted surface
Failing to fill grain adequately allows shellac to sink into the open pores as it sets.
Let the polish harden, rub it down with silicon-carbide paper wrapped round a sanding block and re-polish until the pores are filled flush with shellac.

Blushing
Moisture trapped in the polish gives shellac a cloudy appearance soon after it is applied. This can be caused by humidity during polishing, or perhaps a water stain was not allowed to dry out adequately. Alternatively, the wood itself was left slightly damp.
Because blushing usually penetrates to the wood, the usual recourse is to strip the shellac and re-polish.

Blooming
A cloudy deposit, similar to the bloom found on the skins of grapes, can occur on shellac, whatever its age.
Use a rag barely dampened with water to wipe blooming from the surface, then rub it dry with a duster or paper towel.

Polishing disturbs previous layers
Attempting to apply fresh shellac before previous coats have time to harden smears the polish.
Let each application dry for at least 30 minutes and put the work aside overnight to allow each coat to harden thoroughly (see page 57).

Scars
If the rubber is allowed to come to rest on the surface of the polish, it will leave an imprint of the fabric in the shellac.
Leave the polish to harden overnight, then sand out the scar with silicon-carbide paper. Don't concentrate too much on a small area, or you will wear a pale-coloured patch in the finish.

Ridges in the polish
Ridges will be raised by applying too much pressure to a slightly overcharged rubber.
Treat as for scars.

Runs
Shellac polish will run or 'curtain' just like paint that is applied too thickly without brushing out. This will most likely occur when thinned shellac is being applied, or the rubber or paintbrush is passed across raised mouldings or against a sharp edge.
Don't attempt to spread runs while the polish is still soft. Let it harden, then treat as for rubber scars.

Scratches
If you find that the act of polishing is scratching coats applied previously, check the sole of the rubber for specks of dust or grit. Remake the rubber if you notice a seam running across the sole. A rubber made from synthetic-fibre cloth may also scratch the surface of the polish.
Make sure you wipe the work after rubbing down, and check that you do not press a freshly charged rubber against a dirty surface (see page 55). Sand out scratches and other blemishes when the shellac has hardened overnight.

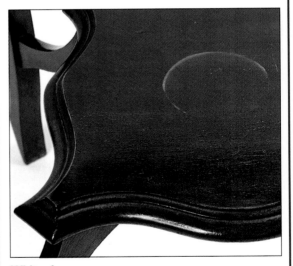

White rings
Circular white stains are caused by the damp base of a vase or glass left in contact with a French-polished surface. Alcohol and heat will have a similar effect.
There are a number of solutions to this problem (see page 30), including burnishing with a proprietary finish reviver, car-paint cleaner or liquid metal polish.

CHAPTER 5

Modern production methods have made available a large range of varnishes and lacquers, each with its own specific properties – durability, weather-resistance, ease of application, drying speed, and so on. Such is their versatility, there is almost certainly a varnish or lacquer that will meet your requirements.

VARNISH & LACQUER

A FINISH FOR EVERY SITUATION

At one time, the terms 'lacquer' and 'varnish' were used to describe specific finishes. Lacquer was for the most part a clear coating that dried quickly by evaporation of the solvent, whereas a conventional varnish was a mixture of resins, oil and solvent that dried by a combination of evaporation and oxidation. Nowadays, a great many finishes are so complex that they no longer fit exactly into either category, but manufacturers have continued to use the familiar terms so as not to disorientate their customers. As a consequence, the labels 'lacquer' and 'varnish' have become interchangeable; to avoid further confusion, the terms used here are those that you are most likely to encounter when buying wood finishes.

The bulk of varnishes and lacquers are clear to amber-coloured finishes, designed primarily to protect the wood and accentuate its natural grain pattern. There are also modified finishes that contain coloured dyes or pigments.

Clear polyurethane varnish is a tough and attractive finish for all interior wood surfaces

Oil varnishes

Traditional oil varnish is composed of fossilized tree resins blended with linseed oil and thinned with turpentine. In the manufacture of modern oil varnishes, these natural resins have been superseded by synthetic ones, such as phenolic, alkyd and polyurethane resins, with white spirit as the solvent.

Oil varnishes, frequently referred to as solvent-based varnishes, dry as a result of oxidation. After the solvent has evaporated, the oil absorbs oxygen from the air, chemically changing the varnish in such a way that applying white spirit does not soften the dried film.

Grained softwood door protected with exterior-grade varnish

Floor sealers are especially hardwearing clear varnishes

The ratio of oil to resin has an effect on the properties of the varnish. Varnishes with a high percentage of oil, known as long oil varnishes, are relatively tough, flexible and water-resistant, making them suitable for finishing exterior woodwork. Short oil varnishes, made with less oil and a higher proportion of resin, dry more quickly and with a harder film than long oil varnishes, and can be polished to a gloss finish. These are also called rubbing varnishes, and are classed as interior woodwork finishes.

The choice of resin also affects the characteristics of a varnish. Exterior-grade varnishes, for example, are often made from alkyd resin blended with tung oil to provide resilience and weather resistance. Manufacturers adopt terms such as spar varnish, marine varnish or yacht varnish to describe superior-quality exterior finishes that will cope with polluted urban environments and coastal climates. Polyurethane resin is favoured for interior oil varnishes, including floor sealers, which need to be tough enough to resist hard knocks and abrasion.

Oil varnishes are supplied ready for use, except for those containing pigments or matting agents, which need to be stirred first (see page 66).

Spirit varnishes

Spirit varnish is manufactured from natural resins, most often shellac, dissolved in meths. It dries quickly by evaporation of the meths, but the film can be softened again by applying the solvent. A spirit varnish has a higher proportion of shellac than a brushing shellac or French polish. Spirit varnishes are seldom used for wood finishing these days, but they are useful when sealing creosoted wood before painting it.

Two-pack polyurethane varnish

In order for this varnish to set hard, the user is required to mix in a precise amount of isocyanate curing agent just prior to application. The result is a clear, tough finish that is better than standard oil varnish in terms of durability and resistance to heat, alcohol and other chemicals. Its one real disadvantage is that, during the curing process, the varnish exudes extremely unpleasant fumes that can be injurious to health, especially to people who suffer from any form of respiratory illness. Consequently, many countries have banned the use of two-pack polyurethane varnishes except in controlled industrial premises fitted with adequate exhaust ventilation.

Protective wood stains (right)

Available as solvent-based and water-based finishes, protective wood stains fall somewhere between exterior varnish and paints. Most are translucent wood-coloured or pastel-shade finishes, but some are completely opaque. These finishes, which should not be confused with genuine penetrating wood stains (see pages 42–3), provide colour and protection for exterior doors and window frames.

For perfect adhesion, wood stains should be applied to bare wood or to previously stained joinery that has been washed thoroughly. Although you usually have to strip conventional varnish or paint, some stains are made to obliterate old paintwork. (See also page 47.)

Acrylic varnishes (above)

The most recently developed wood varnishes are composed of acrylic resins dispersed in water to form an emulsion. The varnish is milky white when applied; it becomes a clear transparent finish after going through a two-stage evaporative process.

Acrylic varnish contains a small percentage of solvents known as coalescing agents which, after the water has evaporated, fuse the particles of resin into a cured film. This process can only take place in a relatively warm, dry atmosphere. In very humid or damp conditions, the coalescing agents may evaporate in advance of the water, leaving a film that cannot set properly. Once it has set, however, the varnish is impervious to water; it can be softened with cellulose thinner if necessary.

Acrylic varnishes have many advantages over solvent-based finishes. They are non-toxic and practic-ally odourless, and dry so fast that you can complete most tasks in a single day. There's no risk of fire, and you can wash out your brushes in ordinary tap water.

Varnish stains (below)

Tinted solvent-based and acrylic finishes allow you to varnish and colour the wood in one operation. Varnish stains are made in various translucent colours, mostly formulated to imitate common wood species; some ranges also include pastel shades. (See also page 47.)

Cold-cure lacquers

Cold-cure lacquers, which set hard by a process known as cross-polymerization, require the addition of an acid catalyst to start the reaction. When cured, the molecules of resin are bonded chemically, forming an extremely tough, non-reversible film which is highly resistant to solvents, heat and abrasion. Because cold-cure lacquers do not rely on evaporation of the solvent or on oxidation for setting, they can be applied in relatively thick coats.

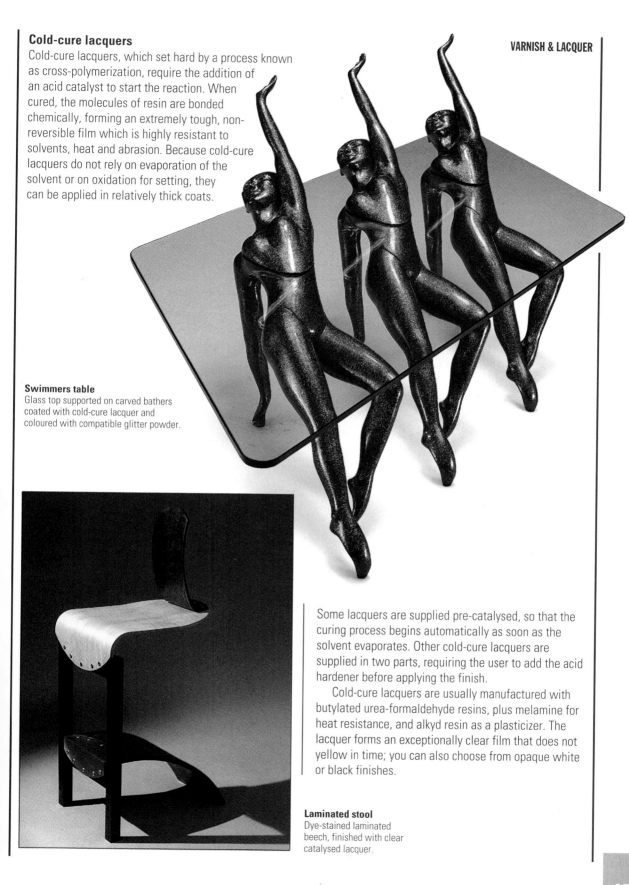

Swimmers table
Glass top supported on carved bathers coated with cold-cure lacquer and coloured with compatible glitter powder.

Some lacquers are supplied pre-catalysed, so that the curing process begins automatically as soon as the solvent evaporates. Other cold-cure lacquers are supplied in two parts, requiring the user to add the acid hardener before applying the finish.

Cold-cure lacquers are usually manufactured with butylated urea-formaldehyde resins, plus melamine for heat resistance, and alkyd resin as a plasticizer. The lacquer forms an exceptionally clear film that does not yellow in time; you can also choose from opaque white or black finishes.

Laminated stool
Dye-stained laminated beech, finished with clear catalysed lacquer.

PROPERTIES OF VARNISH AND LACQUER

Manufacturers are able to vary the formulae of varnishes and lacquers to give them whatever properties are required for a particular need. Listed below are the characteristics most likely to be included in sales literature or user instructions.

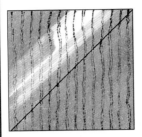

Finish – gloss, satin, matt

Varnishes and lacquers dry to a gloss finish, except when matting agents have been included to make them semi-gloss (satin) or completely matt when set. Most manufacturers make a range of varnishes or lacquers in all three; when a varnish stain, for example, is only available in one finish, you can modify it by coating over it with the appropriate clear varnish.

Clarity and colour

Most varnishes and lacquers are transparent finishes that enhance the colour of the wood without masking the grain pattern. Even finishes described as perfectly clear will darken wood slightly; water has a similar effect. Varnish stains and protective wood stains, which contain pigments or dyes, impose a completely different colour on the wood.

Non-yellowing

Oil varnishes are prone to darkening or turning yellow with age. Both acrylic varnish and cold-cure lacquer retain their clarity.

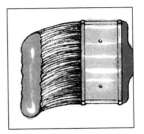

Viscosity

Varnishes and lacquers are usually liquid in consistency, but some, which are described as thixotropic or non-drip, are supplied as a thick gel that flows when brushed onto the work.

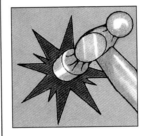

Durability

Modern varnishes and lacquers that can take a great deal of wear and tear are described as being resistant to scratches, abrasion and impact.

Heat resistance

The term heat-resistant implies that you can place hot plates or dishes onto a varnished or lacquered surface without damaging the finish.

Water resistance

A water-resistant coating will not absorb moisture or be stained by spilled water.

Solvent resistance
A solvent-resistant coating will not be softened or stained when subjected to solvents, including alcohol.

Weather resistance
All exterior-grade finishes are weather-resistant. They form a flexible coating that does not flake or crack and is ultra-violet (UV) resistant, thus preventing the wood from fading.

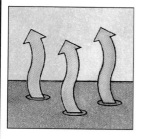

Microporous or water-vapour permeable
Terms used to describe an exterior varnish or protective wood stain that repels rainwater, yet allows moisture vapour to permeate.

Low odour
The low-solvent content of acrylic varnishes makes them practically odourless. There is also a reduced health risk when using low-solvent finishes and they are less harmful to the environment.

Toxicity
Manufacturers are bound by law to include advice on the effects of swallowing a finish or breathing its fumes. Regulations on the use of wood finishes for children's furniture and toys are especially rigorous.

Flammability
Solvent-based wood finishes exude flammable vapours. Acrylic varnishes and other water-based products are non-flammable.

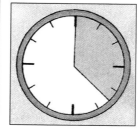

Drying and setting times
Manufacturers invariably quote the period of time it takes for a finish to be 'touch dry', and a much longer setting time, after which it can be re-coated. Drying and setting times of different wood finishes vary a great deal. Although a fast drying time enables you to complete a job quickly, a slow-setting varnish allows more time to spread the finish evenly without leaving brushstrokes. There is, however, a greater chance of airborne dust becoming embedded in a slow-setting finish.

BRUSHING VARNISH

You can spray varnishes onto wood – except for those that are thixotropic – but it is cheaper and more convenient for most amateur woodworkers to apply varnish with a paintbrush. Provided you use good-quality equipment and work patiently, you can achieve perfect results.

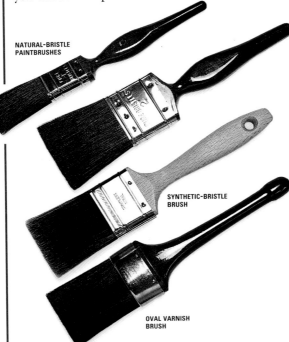

NATURAL-BRISTLE PAINTBRUSHES

SYNTHETIC-BRISTLE BRUSH

OVAL VARNISH BRUSH

Choosing brushes

Any good-quality paintbrush is suitable for applying oil varnish, but natural-bristle brushes that spread the finish well without shedding loose bristles are the best choice. There are also oval-shape varnish brushes, specially designed for greater carrying capacity and improved edge control.

Use synthetic-bristle brushes to apply water-based acrylic varnish. Most varnish manufacturers recommend nylon brushes.

Choose a 50mm (2in) brush for general work and a 25mm (1in) cutting-in brush for varnishing glazing bars and narrow mouldings. A 100mm (4in) brush will be helpful when varnishing floors, but using a brush wider than that becomes tiring after a while.

Whatever brushes you decide to use, reserve them for varnishing woodwork so that they do not become contaminated with specks of dry paint.

When varnishing a floor, consider using a paint roller attached to a long extension handle.

1 Preparing a new brush

Before you use a brand-new brush to apply oil varnish, flex it against the palm of your hand to tease out any loose bristles.

2 Soaking the bristles

Prepare the new brush by soaking the bristles in linseed oil for about 24 hours. If you stand the brush on end in a jar of oil, the bristles will become splayed and useless. Instead, suspend the brush from a short length of stiff wire pushed through a small hole drilled just above the metal ferrule.

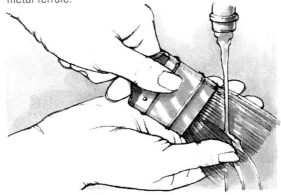

3 Washing out oil

Squeeze excess oil from the bristles, then brush back and forth on clean brown paper or cardboard. Rinse the brush in white spirit and wash it in hot soapy water. When the brush is dry, it is ready for use.

Cleaning and storing brushes

Brushes used for acrylic varnish should be washed immediately in clean water. If they are left to become hard, use cellulose thinner to soften the varnish.

Between applications of oil varnish, suspend the brush in water to keep the bristles soft. Before using it again, blot the brush with paper towelling. When the work is finished, rinse the brush with white spirit, then wash the bristles in hot water and detergent.

Re-shape the wet brush and wrap the bristles in brown paper. Slip an elastic band over the ferrule to hold the paper in place. Lay the brush flat on a shelf, or suspend it from a wall-hung wire rack.

Decanting varnish

Gently stir matt, satin or tinted varnish until you can feel there is no sediment left at the bottom of the container. Thixotropic varnish does not need to be stirred.

You can take varnish straight from the can, but it pays to decant just enough for your immediate needs into a clean paint kettle; replace the can lid to seal in the rest of the varnish. Stretch a length of wire across the top of the kettle to support your brush temporarily.

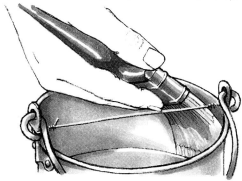

Loading the brush

Dip the first third of the bristles into the varnish; when a brush is overloaded, varnish can set hard in the roots of the bristles, reducing their flexibility. Press the loaded bristles against the side of the kettle to squeeze out excess varnish that might drip from the brush; it is not good practice to drag the bristles across the rim of the kettle, as this tends to create air bubbles.

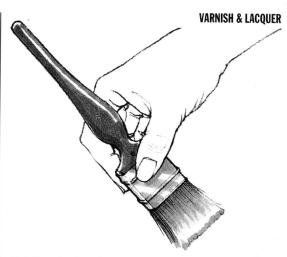

Holding the brush

There are no hard-and-fast rules about how to hold a paintbrush, but when using the pen grip you can move the brush in any direction simply by flexing your wrist. Grip the ferrule between your thumb and fingertips.

PREPARING WOOD

Work in a warm, dry, dust-free atmosphere. However, remember to ventilate the workshop, particularly when applying solvent-based finishes. Don't wear dusty work clothes, or woollen sweaters that could shed fibres.

New or bare wood

Make sure the work is clean, smooth, and free from grease or wax. Wipe oily hardwoods with a cloth dampened with white spirit.

As a precaution, seal stripped wood with sanding sealer to prevent residues of silicone oil from wax polishes contaminating the varnish (see page 26), but always check first with manufacturers' instructions, to ensure that the varnish you are using will set when applied over sanding sealer.

Previously varnished wood

Strip badly chipped or flaking varnish (see pages 31–5). Wash sound varnish to remove dirt and traces of grease. Key gloss varnish with fine wet-and-dry abrasive paper.

Exterior woodwork

Exterior varnishes should be applied on a warm, dry day, preferably after a spell of dry weather. Acrylic varnishes are especially sensitive to levels of humidity and temperature (see page 64).

APPLYING VARNISH

There are no special skills to master when applying solvent-based or acrylic varnishes. However, a few basic procedures can help avoid some of the less obvious pitfalls.

Varnishing a flat panel
Supporting a large panel horizontally on a pair of trestles makes varnishing marginally easier, but there are few problems with finishing a hinged door or fixed panel, provided you guard against the varnish running.

1 Applying a sealer coat of oil varnish
Thin oil varnish by about 10 per cent when applying a first sealer coat to bare wood. You can brush it onto the wood, but some woodworkers prefer to rub it into the grain with a soft cloth.

2 Rubbing down the first coat
Leave the sealer coat to harden overnight, then hold the work in a good source of light to inspect the varnished surface. Rub it down lightly in the direction of the grain, using fine wet-and-dry paper dipped in water. Wipe the surface clean, using a cloth moistened with white spirit, and dry it with a paper towel.

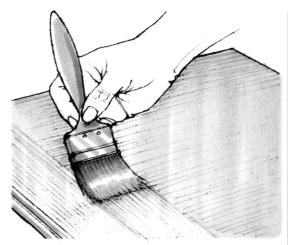

3 Brushing full-strength varnish
Paint oil varnish onto the wood, brushing first with the grain then across it to spread the finish evenly. Always brush towards the area you have just finished, to blend the wet edges. It pays to work at a fairly brisk pace; varnish begins to set after about 10 minutes, and re-brushing it tends to leave permanent brushmarks. Finally 'lay off' along the grain with very light strokes, using just the tips of the bristles to leave a smoothly varnished surface. When varnishing vertical surfaces, lay off with upward strokes of the brush.

Two full-strength coats of oil varnish should be sufficient; for a perfect finish, rub down lightly between each hardened coat.

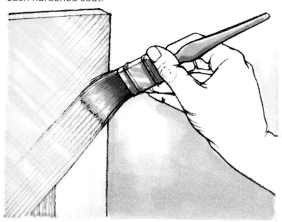

Varnishing edges
As you approach the edges of a panel, brush outwards away from the centre. If you flex the bristles back against the sharp arris, you will cause varnish to dribble down the edge.

It is best to blend in the edges of a workpiece as the work progresses, but if that proves troublesome, try varnishing the edges of a panel first and letting them dry. When you coat the flat surfaces, wipe runs from the edges with a rag.

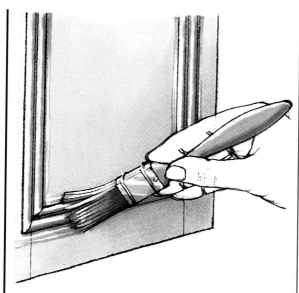

Varnishing mouldings

Flexing a brush across a moulding usually causes a teardrop of varnish to run down the surface. Avoid this by brushing along the moulding only.

When finishing a panelled door, varnish the mouldings first and then varnish the panel, brushing out from each corner towards the centre.

Matting a gloss varnish

Matt and satin oil varnishes have very finely textured surfaces that serve to scatter the light. These look perfect, but you can achieve a smoother-feeling surface on components such as wooden chair arms or a table top by rubbing down a gloss varnish to a matt finish.

Rub the varnish with 000-grade steel wool dipped in wax polish. Leave the wax to harden, then burnish it with a soft duster.

APPLYING ACRYLIC VARNISH

Many of the techniques employed when applying oil varnish are just as relevant to the application of acrylic varnish. The aim is still to acquire a flat, even coating without runs or brushmarks, but the chemical properties of acrylic varnish make it behave slightly differently from oil varnish.

Grain-raising characteristics

When a piece of wood absorbs water, its fibres swell and stand up proud of the surface. Because it is water-based, acrylic varnish has the same effect, making the final finish less than perfect. The solution is either to wet the wood first, and sand it smooth before applying acrylic varnish (see page 20), or to sand the first coat of varnish with fine wet-and-dry paper dipped in water before re-coating the work. Wipe up the dust with a cloth dampened with water; a tack rag may leave oily deposits that will spoil the next coat of acrylic varnish.

Problems with rust

Applying any water-based finish over unprotected steel or iron fittings, including woodscrews and nails, will cause them to rust. Either remove metal fittings before you varnish the work, or protect them with a coat of de-waxed transparent shellac (see page 53).

Don't use steel wool to rub down acrylic varnish; tiny slivers of metal that get caught in the grain may rust, creating black spots on the wood. Use copper wool or an abrasive nylon-fibre pad (see page 17).

Applying the varnish

Acrylic varnish must be applied liberally, first by brushing across the grain, then laying off evenly as described for applying oil varnish (see opposite).

Acrylic varnish dries in only 20 to 30 minutes, so you need to work fast, especially on a hot day, to avoid leaving permanent brushmarks in the finish.

You can apply a second coat after two hours. A total of three coats is sufficient for maximum protection.

APPLYING COLD-CURE LACQUER

This is a very different finish from conventional varnish. Although cold-cure lacquer is no more difficult to apply, it is important to be aware of how the curing process can be affected by inadequate preparation and inappropriate procedures.

Mixing cold-cure lacquer

Mix recommended amounts of hardener and lacquer in a glass jar or polythene container. Metal containers and other plastics may react with the hardener, preventing the lacquer from curing.

Once mixed, some cold-cure lacquers are usable for about three days. However, you can extend the pot life to about a week by covering the jar with polythene, held in place with an elastic band. This type of lacquer will last even longer if you keep the sealed container, clearly marked, in a refrigerator.

Brush care

Apply cold-cure lacquer with any good-quality paintbrush. It can also be sprayed, and can even be applied to large areas with a plastic-foam paint roller.

Once polymerization is complete, cold-cure lacquer becomes insoluble, so wash brushes in special lacquer thinner as soon as the work is complete. The brush can be left suspended in the mixed lacquer between coats, provided the whole container, including the brush, is wrapped in polythene.

Preparing the surface

As with any wood finish, the work must be smooth and clean; remove every trace of wax, which might prevent the lacquer curing. Any wood dye applied to the work must be compatible with the acid catalyst in the lacquer, so check the manufacturers' recommendations before colouring the wood.

Applying cold-cure lacquer

Adequate ventilation is important, especially when you are lacquering a floor, but keep the workshop warm.

Brush on lacquer liberally, using a flowing action and blending in wet edges as you go. Apply it relatively thickly, taking care to avoid runs or sagging.

The lacquer will be touch dry in about 15 minutes; apply a second coat after about an hour. If a third coat is required, apply it the following day.

There is no need to rub down between coats, except to correct blemishes. It you use stearated abrasives (see page 18), wipe the sanded surface with special lacquer thinner.

Modifying the finish

To achieve a perfect gloss finish, let the last coat harden for a few days, then sand it smooth with wet-and-dry paper and water until the surface appears matt all over; a shiny patch indicates a hollow. Using a burnishing cream on a slightly damp cloth, buff the surface to a high gloss, and then rub it with a duster.

To create a satin finish, rub the hardened lacquer with 000-grade steel wool lubricated with wax polish. Use coarser steel wool for a matt finish.

CELLULOSE LACQUER

Cellulose lacquer dries solely by evaporation of its solvent, leaving a film that will re-dissolve readily when cellulose thinner is applied to the surface. As a result, each successive coat partially dissolves and melds with the previous application, eventually becoming one integral film of lacquer.

This is a water-clear finish that hardly changes the colour of the wood. It also sets very rapidly – it is re-coatable after only 30 minutes – which all but eliminates the problem of dust contamination.

Cellulose lacquer is not as resistant to heat, water or abrasion as polyurethane varnish or cold-cure lacquer, for example, but it does compare favourably with shellac polish. Ventilation is essential when applying cellulose lacquer, and you should wear an approved respirator (see page 125). The lacquer is highly flammable.

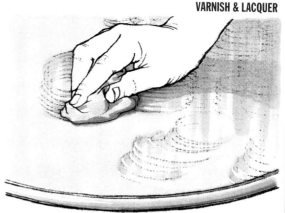

1 Sealing the work
Using a cloth pad, apply a sealer coat of lacquer diluted by 50 per cent with cellulose thinner.

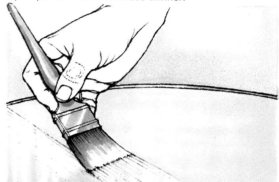

2 Applying full-strength lacquer
Brush on additional full-strength coats, laying on the lacquer with a flowing action. Hold the brush at a shallow angle to the surface, applying the finish with long, straight, overlapping strokes. Don't spread the lacquer like varnish or you run the risk of leaving visible brushmarks in the rapidly setting finish.

Spraying and brushing lacquer
Conventional cellulose lacquer dries so quickly that spraying is the only practicable method of application (see pages 80–8). If your workshop is not equipped with the required spray gun, compressor and ventilation system, use a specially formulated lacquer made with slow-evaporating solvent so that it can be brushed on to the wood.

3 Burnishing the finish
After about an hour, rub down the final coat of lacquer to remove any minor blemishes. You can use fine wet-and-dry paper or self-lubricating silicon-carbide paper. Rub to the required finish, using burnishing cream.

FAULTS AND REMEDIES

The following is a check list of problems that are commonly encountered when using varnish and cold-cure lacquer.

VARNISH
Runs and sagging
Excess varnish runs or sags if not brushed out sufficiently.
Wipe upwards against the flow of fresh runs, using an unloaded brush.

Rub down runs that have set hard, using wet-and-dry paper dipped in water. If practicable, first pare down hardened runs with a sharp chisel, to minimize rubbing down.

Embedded dust particles
There is very little you can do to prevent the occasional speck of dust from settling on wet varnish.
If the varnish is still wet, pick up a speck of dust with a pointed toothpick; the varnish will flow back to fill the hollow, forming a smooth coat.

If the varnish has begun to set, leave embedded dust until the next day, then rub the surface down with wet-and-dry paper.

Embedded bristles
Even the best brush will shed the occasional bristle.
Scoop up a dropped bristle with the tip of the brush. If you don't notice a detached bristle until the varnish has set, pick it out with the point of a sharp knife and rub down with wet-and-dry paper.

Varnish rolls up into tiny balls and clogs abrasive paper when rubbing down
The varnish has not been left to harden sufficiently. If the original coat was applied too thickly, it may be touch dry but still soft beneath. As a test, press your thumbnail into the varnish; if it leaves an impression, the varnish is too soft to rub down.
Leave the work for another 24 hours and rub down with wet-and-dry paper.

Brushstrokes set permanently in the varnish
Marks are caused by brushing back over a coating that has just begun to set.
If you accidentally brush into setting varnish, don't attempt to rectify the damage; it simply gets worse. Leave it to dry overnight, then rub down.

Cissing or fish-eye
Traces of silicone wax left in the pores of the wood can repel a finish, resulting in miniature craters.
See page 88.

Acrylic varnish dries to a white powder
If acrylic varnish is applied in damp or humid conditions, the coalescing agents evaporate before the water does, and the varnish dries to a white powder.
Brush the powder off the surface and re-varnish.

Acrylic varnish dries too fast to be brushed out effectively
Hot, dry weather reduces the drying time of water-based varnish considerably.
Dilute the varnish by about 10 per cent.

COLD-CURE LACQUER
Film does not dry within expected time
Failing to remove all traces of grease or wax from the wood, using a liming wax to fill the grain, adding insufficient hardener, and applying the finish in a temperature of less than 19°C (65°F) can all delay the drying process.
If you leave the workpiece in a warm room, the lacquer will dry eventually, but it may take several days. You can protect a lacquered floor with a sheet of polythene until the finish has set hard.

Second coat of lacquer wrinkles or blisters
The solvent in the lacquer affects an underlying coat that has not set hard.
Leave the workpiece in a warm room for a few days.

Lacquer appears misty after burnishing
It is not possible to burnish lacquer to a high gloss until it has set hard.
Re-burnish after leaving the work in a warm room for several days.

Poor adhesion
Using stearated abrasives to rub down cold-cure lacquer leaves dust that can affect the adhesion of subsequent coats.
Wipe up dust with a cloth dampened with the special lacquer thinner before applying fresh lacquer.

CHAPTER 6

Paints and varnishes are made from similar resins and solvents, and have many characteristics in common. The one real difference is that paints contain coloured pigments that obliterate the grain pattern, and as a result are more often used for finishing inexpensive hardwood joinery, softwoods and boards.

PAINT FINISHES

PRIMERS, UNDERCOATS AND TOP COATS

When applying a protective body of varnish or lacquer, the same material is used for each coat, but conventional paintwork is a combination of three slightly different paints – a single coat of primer effectively seals the wood and provides a surface to which subsequent coats will adhere well, two to three coats of dense matt undercoat form the protective layer, and a colourful top coat provides a satin or gloss finish.

PRIMERS
Solvent-based wood primer
You can choose from white or pink primer, depending on which will work best with the colour and tone of subsequent coats of paint. A combination of red lead and white lead accounted for the colour of traditional pink primer; pink remains the preferred colour, even though lead is no longer added to non-trade paints. Leave solvent-based primers to dry overnight.

Acrylic wood primer
Water-based acrylic primers, which can be used as a base for oil or acrylic paints, dry in about four hours. Except for those specially formulated for finishing metals, water-based paints cause steel fittings to rust unless they are protected with a coat of transparent shellac (see page 53).

Aluminium wood primer
Solvent-based primers that contain aluminium particles contribute towards good weather resistance.
Aluminium primers are also recommended for sealing all hardwoods, especially oily ones, resinous softwoods and timber treated with dark-coloured wood preserver. They are also the primers to choose if you are painting woodwork that has been scorched while being stripped with heat.

UNDERCOATS
Solvent-based undercoat
Undercoat, which is formulated to obliterate wood grain and primer, dries to an even, matt finish, and can be rubbed down with wet-and-dry paper to a perfectly flat surface. Solvent-based undercoats, which are usually available in white, grey and a limited range of colours, should be left to harden overnight.

Acrylic undercoat
Water-based acrylic undercoats dry so fast you can complete the average job, including the top coat, in a single day; some paints are ready for another coat after only one hour. A few manufacturers market a single acrylic paint that can be used for both priming and undercoating. Acrylic undercoat can be overlaid with solvent-based or water-based top coats.

Bare wood
Grain raised and sanded smooth.

Primer
Seals the wood and provides the ideal base for other paints.

Undercoat
Two to three coats obliterate primer and build a protective body of paint.

Top coat
Final paint finish provides a colourful, wipe-clean surface.

TOP COATS
Solvent-based paint

A top coat forms the final decorative surface and is generally available as a high-gloss finish or with a subtle satin sheen. Although few paint manufacturers distinguish between exterior and interior finishes, gloss paint is generally more weather-resistant than satin.

Non-drip thixotropic paints do not require stirring unless the medium has settled out during storage, in which case allow the paint to gel again before using it. Solvent-based top coats are touch-dry within two to four hours, and set completely overnight.

One-coat paint

Solvent-based one-coat gloss and satin paints do not require separate undercoats, thus saving time. They are made to a creamy consistency, with a relatively high proportion of pigments. One-coat paints are especially useful for obliterating old paintwork and strong colours. They must be applied liberally to be fully effective, and should not be spread too thinly.

Acrylic paint

Water-based acrylic paints are similar to acrylic varnishes in many ways. The most obvious similarity is that both set by evaporation of the water, followed by coalescing agents that fuse the resin into a hard film. This means that acrylic paints may not set satisfactorily if they are applied on a cold damp day or during a period of high humidity (see page 64).

Although acrylic paints are available as gloss and satin finishes, water-based paints are not quite as glossy as the solvent-based variety.

Acrylic paints dry quickly; they are also non-toxic, non-flammable, and practically odourless. Check with the manufacturer's recommendations to make sure that a particular acrylic paint is suitable for finishing exterior joinery.

Milk paint

Formulated to recreate an authentic nineteenth-century finish, milk paints are supplied as coloured powders for mixing with water. They are made from milk protein, lime and clay, plus a subtle range of earth pigments. Milk paints dry with a matt finish, but can be burnished if you prefer a satin sheen. For additional protection, apply a coat of clear varnish.

These paints are aimed primarily at restorers, but they are equally suitable for new work. You don't need to prime bare wood, but a special primer is available for use on ready-painted surfaces.

Metallic paint

Manufacturers offer a range of gold, silver, copper and bronze paints, primarily for finishing picture frames, boxes, and other small decorative objects. They are not protective coatings in their own right, but you can cover them with slightly thinned clear varnish if the object is to be handled.

Metallic paints must be stirred thoroughly before use, and applied with a soft paintbrush.

APPLYING PAINT FINISHES

Compared with spraying, applying paint with a brush or pad is a relatively slow process and one where it is difficult to achieve the same quality of finish. However, since it avoids the cost of specialized equipment, and because almost everyone has used a paintbrush, painting by hand is still most woodworkers' preferred method of applying paint finishes.

Choosing a good-quality brush
Check the quality of a brush by fanning the bristles with your fingers. The bristles should be densely packed, and they should spring back to shape readily. The bunch of bristles, known as the filling, should be glued firmly into the metal ferrule which, in turn, must be fixed securely to the wooden or plastic handle. A 50mm (2in) brush is ideal for general paintwork, and you will need a 25mm (1in) brush for precise work.

Cleaning pads and brushes
As soon as you have finished painting, blot a pad or paintbrush on a layer of old newspaper, rinse it in white spirit, then wash the bristles or pile with hot water and detergent. Wash out brushes used with acrylic paint immediately with water. Re-shape clean brushes and wrap them for storage (see page 69).

Soften hardened oil paint by soaking the bristles in proprietary brush cleaner or paint stripper, then wash the brush thoroughly with soap and water. Cellulose thinner will soften hardened acrylic paint.

Brushes, paint pads and rollers
When choosing brushes for painting, the same rules apply as for varnishing (see page 68). The best brushes for solvent-based paints are made from tough, resilient hog hair. Slightly cheaper ones are a mixture of natural bristles, usually hog, ox or horse hair. Synthetic bristles mimic natural hair, tapering to a tip which is flagged; they divide at the very tip into even finer filaments that hold a finish well. Use these for water-based paints.

Mohair-lined, foamed-plastic pads are the modern equivalent of the paintbrush for finishing large flat surfaces. Some painters also use a smaller version, known as a sash pad, for glazing bars, spindles and mouldings. Gently brush a new pad with a clothes brush to remove any loose filaments from the pile.

You could use a small mohair roller to paint a large door or panel.

NARROW PAINTBRUSH
FOR PRECISE WORK

SYNTHETIC-BRISTLE
PAINTBRUSH

SASH PAD

GENERAL-PURPOSE
NATURAL-BRISTLE BRUSH

MOHAIR-LINED
PAINT PAD

LOADING PAINT PADS
Paint pads are sold with a special tray that has a roller built into one end. As you draw the pad across the roller, paint is distributed evenly across the pile.

Pouring paint into a kettle

Pour just enough paint for your needs into a plastic paint kettle to make loading a paintbrush easier (see page 69).

If using paint left over from a previous job, it pays to filter it through a piece of muslin or old tights stretched over the kettle; don't, however, do this with thixotropic paint. If old paint has skinned over, cut round the edge with a knife and lift out the skin with a stick before filtering the paint.

Sealing a can of paint

When re-sealing the can, always wipe paint from the rim with a cloth pad and tap down the lid, using a hammer and a block of wood. Shaking the can afterwards helps prevent a skin forming over the paint.

APPLYING PAINTS

Make sure the work is clean and sanded smooth before brushing on the first coat of paint. Acrylic primer and milk paint are water-based, so be sure to raise the grain before applying them (see page 20).

Although paints are opaque, they will not hide the effects of resinous knots which will eventually discolour the paintwork. Seal suspect knots with shellac-based knotting (see page 51) before painting with solvent-based or acrylic paints.

Strip off chipped or flaking paint (see pages 31–5), and wash sound paintwork to remove dirt and traces of grease. Key gloss paint with fine abrasive paper.

Choosing your moment

Paint exterior woodwork during warm dry weather. Avoid working on a windy day, or airborne dust might ruin your paintwork.

Applying solvent-based paint

When using conventional oil paint, apply a primer and a minimum of two undercoats, followed by a single top coat. Rub down between coats with wet-and-dry paper, wiping off the sludge with a cloth dampened with white spirit.

Spread the paint with vertical and sideways strokes, laying off with the tips of the bristles for a smooth finish. Avoid visible brushmarks and runs as described for applying varnish (see pages 70–1).

There is no need to spread thixotropic paint; apply it fairly liberally, smooth it out using virtually parallel strokes, then lay off lightly.

Applying acrylic paint

Brush on water-based paint as you would acrylic varnish (see page 71), blending wet edges quickly.

SPRAYING FINISHES

Spraying wood finishes is not only faster than brushing but, once you have mastered the basics, it also guarantees superior results. Sprayed paint-work, in particular, has a smooth, even quality that is difficult to achieve by any other method, and it is worth spending time developing your technique by practising on scrap wood and boards before you tackle an actual workpiece.

Spraying systems
In industry and building construction, various hands-on and semi-automated systems are employed for spraying anything from furniture to motor cars, and for decorating interior and exterior surfaces. However, amateur wood finishers require a versatile system, and one that is reasonably inexpensive, compact and reliable. For most people, this means using a small electric-powered compressor that delivers pressurized air to a finely adjustable, hand-held spray gun.

Basic spraying equipment can be hired if you don't want to invest a lot of money at one time, but if you are going to the trouble of constructing a spray booth with built-in extraction, you would do best to equip yourself with a suitable system.

Spray guns
All spray guns atomize a fluid finish, depositing it as a fine mist onto the workpiece, where it flows together to form a perfectly even surface coating. Squeezing the trigger allows compressed air to flow through the spray gun, where it is mixed with paint or other finishes drawn from a reservoir that is mounted above or below the gun.

A gravity-feed cup, attached to the top of the gun, will hold up to about half a litre (1 pint) of paint or clear finish. A filter at the base of the cup prevents dirt particles blocking the gun's nozzle. Gravity-feed guns, often made with relatively lightweight plastic reservoirs, are suitable for spraying most wood finishes, but may not be able to cope with heavily pigmented paints.

A suction-feed spray gun is more versatile because it can handle any wood finish, including metallic paints. Compressed air flows through the gun creating a vacuum that draws finish from a reservoir carried below. Suction-feed reservoirs are invariably larger than gravity cups, so require refilling less often. However, a canister that holds up to a litre (2 pints) of paint can make the spray gun unwieldy, and you have to guard against striking the work with the reservoir slung below the gun.

High-volume, low-pressure (HPLV) spray guns are becoming popular for home spraying, as they produce little overspray and paint waste. They can be run with compressed air or continuous air supplied by a turbine.

Gravity-feed spray gun

Suction-feed spray gun

Spray-gun controls

A top-of-the-range gun has sophisticated controls for balancing air pressure, fluid output and spray pattern.

Fluid tip

The fluid tip is where paint and compressed air are brought together. Air escapes from holes surrounding the central nozzle, from which the wood finish emerges. Squeezing the gun's trigger opens the valve that controls the flow of air momentarily before it also withdraws a spring-loaded needle from the nozzle, allowing paint or varnish to flow.

Fluid-output adjuster

A screw mounted at the rear of the spray gun is used to govern how far the needle can be withdrawn from the fluid-tip nozzle in relation to the trigger, thereby regulating the flow of finish from the gun.

Air valve

Air pressure to the gun is set at the compressor, but an adjustment screw fitted to some spray guns allows you to fine-tune the pressure. Adjust air pressure until it is as low as possible while still maintaining effective atomization.

Air-flow adjuster

Another adjustment screw, usually fitted at the back of the gun, controls the amount of air that flows through the fluid tip to the horns. This allows you to modify the spray pattern, from a narrow cone to the maximum width of fan.

FITTING A SUCTION-FEED RESERVOIR

When attaching the reservoir to the spray gun, make sure that the bent pipe that leads to the base of the canister faces towards the nozzle of the gun. This ensures that the pipe will pick up more of the finishing material in the cup when the gun is tilted slightly forward of horizontal (see page 86).

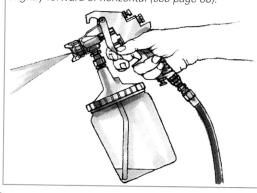

External-mix air cap

The fluid-tip nozzle protrudes from the centre of the air cap. A narrow gap surrounding the nozzle is the outlet for air that is directed into the stream of fluid, atomizing it into extremely fine droplets. Some of the compressed air, diverted to 'horns' mounted on each side of the cap, compresses the spray pattern from cone to fan-shaped.

Matched sets

Although many wood finishers make do with a single combination of air cap, fluid tip and needle, pigmented finishes and metallic paints, for example, may require a different set-up. Spray-gun manufacturers publish guides recommending matched sets of needle, cap and tip for various finishes, compressor sizes and scales of production.

LOCKING RING

AIR CAP

HORN

FLUID -TIP NOZZLE

HORN

AIR-FLOW ADJUSTER

FLUID-OUTPUT ADJUSTER

GRACO MODEL 700

TRIGGER

D.L

AIR VALVE

AIR-SUPPLY HOSE

RESERVOIR

Controls of a suction-feed spray gun

COMPRESSORS

Small portable compressors are designed to work with simple, constant-bleed spray guns that have very basic controls. To operate spray guns with the full range of controls described on page 81, you need a compressor incorporating an air receiver or reservoir, from which compressed air is drawn off through a flexible hose running to the gun.

Choosing a compressor

A typical compressor for the home workshop has a single- or twin-cylinder air pump driven by an electric motor, either by means of a drive belt or, more commonly, direct-coupled as a single unit. Compressed air is pumped into a receiving tank and the motor cuts out when the tank is full. As air is drawn off by the spray gun, the pressure in the tank begins to fall; on its reaching a pre-set level, the motor cuts in to top up the tank again.

Choose a compressor with a 2HP motor that can deliver 8cfm (cubic feet per minute). If space is limited, select a compact unit with a 25 litre (6.5 US gal) air receiver; however, a 50 litre (13 US gal) receiver can cope with a whole range of additional air tools.

Compressors are also rated according to maximum working pressure, typically 120 to 150psi (pounds per square inch). Since you need an operating range of something like 30 to 50psi for spraying and perhaps 80 to 100psi for air tools, the maximum working pressure of most compressors is more than sufficient. Always follow the manufacturers' instructions when setting the air pressure.

MOTOR

FILTER REGULATOR

AIR-HOSE CONNECTION

AIR RECEIVER

DRAIN COCK AT BASE OF RECEIVER

2HP electric compressor

Regulators and filters

Most compressors are manufactured with a built-in regulator to ensure that air is delivered to the spray gun at a constant pressure; a gauge on the instrument records the air pressure, which can be adjusted by turning the regulator valve. The hose is attached by simple quick-fit connectors.

On some models, the regulator incorporates a filter to remove moisture and other contaminants before the air reaches the gun; water droplets collect at the bottom of the reservoir where they can be drained off at regular intervals. If you need to operate with a long hose, it may be necessary to fit a second filter closer to the spray gun to remove any moisture that may have condensed in the line. In-line filter regulators have a drain cock for removing any water collected at that point.

Constructing a spray booth

Spraying is a wasteful process, depositing only about 30 per cent of the paint or varnish onto the work-piece. The rest is lost to the atmosphere as overspray and, if it were not extracted in some way, would fill the workshop with a highly flammable mist of fumes and paint particles. Some woodworkers cope by spraying in the open air or by setting up the work-piece just inside the open doors of a workshop or garage, so that the overspray is directed outside. However, neither situation is entirely satisfactory, and it is better to construct a spray booth fitted with an extractor fan that will in effect collect the overspray, filtering out the solids and depositing the fumes outside the workshop.

Unless you intend to spray water-based finishes only, you need a filtered extractor fan with a shielded motor that prevents sparks igniting solvent fumes. Any switches and light fittings installed in the spray booth must also be explosion-proof.

Building a basic booth

Construct a three-sided box from a softwood frame-work covered with hardboard or MDF panels. Mount the extractor fan in the rear wall of the booth. Line the inside of the booth with sheets of paper that can be replaced after each job.

Arrange a light source above you or on each side of the booth, to avoid throwing your shadow on the work. Light reflected off the back wall will help you judge the condition of the paintwork.

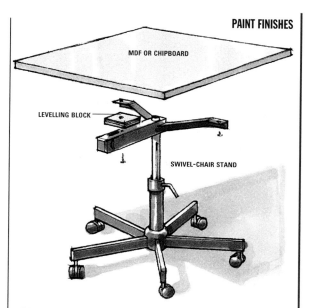

MDF OR CHIPBOARD

LEVELLING BLOCK

SWIVEL-CHAIR STAND

Making a turntable

To avoid being covered with overspray, always position the workpiece between you and the extractor. The easiest way to accomplish this is to make a turntable for the work, so that you can rotate the workpiece to present unfinished surfaces to the spray gun in turn. You can buy proprietary turntables, but it may be cheaper to convert a swivel-chair stand.

SAFETY WHEN SPRAYING

Before you invest too much money on equipment, check with your local authority, fire department and possibly your insurance company to ensure you are able to comply with any requirements or regulations for building a spray booth and operating paint-spraying equipment in your workshop.

● Always work outside or install an approved extractor to remove solvent fumes from the workshop.

● When spraying, wear goggles, overalls and an approved respirator.

● Don't smoke when spraying, and extinguish naked flames in the workshop.

● Don't point a spray gun at yourself or anyone else.

● Disconnect a spray gun from the supply hose before attempting any service or repair work (see page 85).

● Keep a fire blanket and extinguisher close to hand.

ADJUSTING AND TESTING SPRAY GUNS

Adjusting spray equipment to get the best results each time will become automatic with experience, but initially it is worth experimenting with the range of adjustments to see how your particular system operates. Unless you are working with cellulose lacquer, which is usually sold in a sprayable consistency, you will need to dilute the finish with an appropriate solvent.

Thinning wood finishes
Check the manufacturers' recommendations for the ideal ratio of finish to thinner when preparing paint, varnish or cold-cure lacquer. To avoid having to mix a second batch to the same consistency, always make up enough thinned finish to complete the job.

Checking consistency
Stir the thinner into the finish with a wooden stick, then lift out the stick to see how well the diluted finish runs from the tip. If it is still too thick, the finish will drip or run intermittently from the stick, but if it runs smoothly, in a steady continuous stream, the paint or varnish is about ready for spraying. Before spraying a workpiece, test the finish on a practice board – an overdiluted finish will run almost immediately.

Using a viscosity cup
For a more scientific test of consistency, you can run the fluid through a viscosity cup, a type of funnel that will empty at a precise rate when the finish is thinned accurately.

Adjusting the controls
To test the controls of a spray gun, set up a piece of plywood or MDF in the spray booth. Fill the gun's reservoir to the recommended level with paint so that you can see the effects of adjusting the controls.

1 Setting the air pressure
The easiest way to set the required air pressure is to open fully the air valve on the gun's handgrip, then adjust the valve on the compressor's regulator until the gauge reads the required pressure; about 30psi is a good starting point.

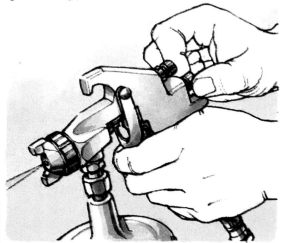

2 Adjusting fluid output
Start with the fluid-output screw fully closed. Aim the gun at the workpiece, holding the nozzle about 200mm (8in) from the surface, and squeeze the trigger. Gradually open the fluid-output adjuster until you begin to wet the surface with paint. If the adjuster is opened too far, too much fluid will be sprayed onto the surface and begin to run.

Maintaining compressors

Drain water from the receiver and filter regulator each day or after every spraying session.

Following the manufacturer's instructions, check the oil level regularly and change the air-intake filter when necessary. Remove accumulated dust from the compressor's cooling fins.

3 Fine-tuning

Experiment with the controls, using the air valve or the regulator to increase and decrease air pressure, and balancing the effects by adjusting the fluid flow.

Another test is to move the gun closer to the work-piece and then bring it away, to gauge when too much fluid is applied to the surface and, conversely, when the paint only settles as a dry dusting. The relative humidity of the atmosphere and the rate at which the thinner evaporates will also affect the quality of finish.

CLEANING A SPRAY GUN

Having to replace a ruined paintbrush is not a disaster, but if you neglect to clean out a spray gun you will be faced with a hefty bill for replacement parts, or even a completely new gun.

As soon as you have finished spraying, empty the reservoir and add thinner. Operate the gun until clean thinner begins to emerge from the nozzle. If you have run out of a specific thinner, cellulose thinner can be used to clean out most modern finishes.

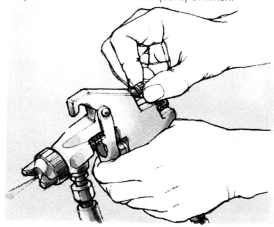

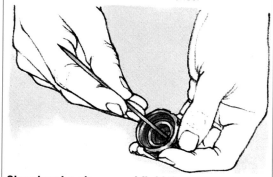

4 Setting the spray pattern

With the air-flow adjuster fully closed, the gun will emit a narrow cone of atomized paint. With the horns set horizontally, gradually open the adjuster, watching how the spray pattern changes to a wide vertical fan. Slacken the locking ring on the air cap, turn the horns to a vertical position and hand-tighten the locking ring again; in this configuration, the gun produces a horizontal, fan-shaped spray pattern.

Cleaning the air cap and fluid tip

Close the valve that delivers air to the hose, squeeze the gun's trigger to clear the hose, then disconnect the spray gun. Remove the air cap so that you can wipe it and the fluid tip clean with a piece of soft rag. Remove any obvious blockages, using a wooden toothpick and the synthetic-bristle brush supplied with the gun. Wipe the inside of the reservoir and the outside of the gun with a rag moistened with thinner.

SPRAYING TECHNIQUES

As a general rule, it is best to apply several thin coats of wood finish, rubbed down between applications with wet-and-dry paper to remove specks of dust and other blemishes. Sprayed finishes tend to become touch-dry relatively quickly, but you will need space to put workpieces aside to harden properly; dampen the floor to keep airborne dust to a minimum.

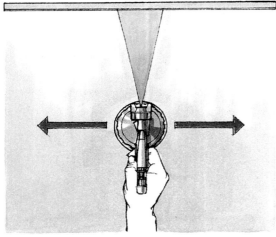

Pointing the gun
To achieve a perfectly even finish, it is important to keep the gun pointed directly at the work. When spraying a wide panel, for example, flex your wrist so that you move the gun on a path parallel to the surface of the work.

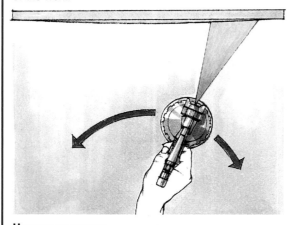

Uneven coverage
If you make the common mistake of swinging the gun in an arc, you will deposit insufficient paint or varnish along each side of the workpiece, leaving a strip of thicker finish down the centre.

Spraying a flat panel
Before spraying a vertical board or panel, adjust the gun to produce a fan-shape spray pattern (see page 85).

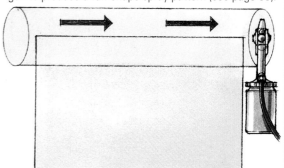

1 Making the first pass
Aligning the nozzle with the top edge of the workpiece, aim the gun to one side of the panel. Squeeze the trigger and make one continuous pass at a steady pace across the panel. Don't release the trigger until the gun is aiming well clear of the panel.

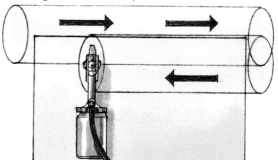

2 Overlapping with the return pass
Squeeze the trigger again and make a second pass in the opposite direction, overlapping the first application by 50 per cent. To coat the entire panel evenly, overlap each subsequent pass in a similar way, squeezing and releasing the trigger at the start and end of each pass; spraying continuously may seem easier, but is very wasteful of paint or varnish.

Spraying a horizontal panel
You may find it easier to lay a small panel flat on your turntable. Working away from you, make overlapping parallel passes, holding the gun at an angle of about 45 degrees to the work.

SPRAYING ASSEMBLED WORKPIECES

Spraying individual components, such as panels, doors or shelves, is relatively straightforward (see opposite), but when you are finishing assembled pieces, work out a sequence that will enable you to coat all surfaces in turn, and will also allow you to move the workpiece without spoiling the finish.

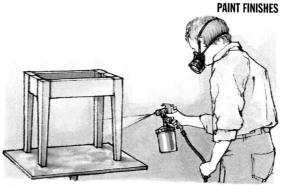

Spraying a table

It is always more convenient to spray a table top and underframe separately. Set the gun to produce a cone-shape spray pattern for finishing narrow legs and rails, spreading the pattern into a fan for spraying the top.

• Spray the underside of the top and put it aside to dry.
• Stand the underframe on the turntable and spray the inside of the legs and rails. When spraying square legs, aim the gun at one corner so that you coat two surfaces at once.
• Spray the outside of the legs and rails.
• Return the table top to the turntable, supporting it on small blocks of wood. Spray the edges all round, then coat the top surface evenly (see opposite).

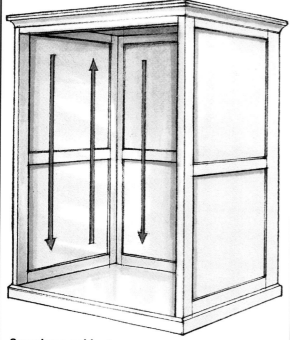

Spraying a cabinet

Finish the doors as individual panels before fitting them to a cabinet. Spray the inside of the cabinet first, trying not to aim the gun directly into a right-angle corner.

Depending on the size of the cabinet, either set the gun to produce a horizontal fan-shape spray pattern (see page 85), or use a cone-shape pattern for finishing interior surfaces.

• Finish the underside of the top panel.
• Spray down one side of the cabinet, then across the back panel.
• Coat the remaining side panel, then complete the interior by spraying the bottom of the cabinet.
• Spray the exterior of the cabinet, treating each panel individually.

Spraying a chair

Set a cone-shape pattern for chair legs and stretcher rails and, if necessary, open it out into a small fan for finishing the seat and back rest.

• Turn the chair upside down on the turntable so that you can spray the insides of the legs and rails.
• Spray the underside of the seat.
• Stand the chair on its feet and spray the outside of the legs and stretcher rails.
• Spray the edges of seat followed by the top surface.
• Finish the inside of armrests and chair back.
• Spin the chair round to coat the outside of the arm-rests and chair back.

FAULTS AND REMEDIES

Brushed-on varnishes, lacquers and paints exhibit certain faults that result from poor preparation or from their sensitivity to temperature or humidity (see pages 74 and 79). You are likely to encounter similar problems when the same finishes are sprayed. The following is a list of problems that are directly related to spraying or that occur most often when a finish is applied with a spray gun.

'Orange peel'
The finish dries with a wrinkled appearance similar to the skin of an orange. In most cases, this is the result of holding the gun too close to the workpiece or of spraying a fluid that has not been diluted sufficiently.
Let the finish harden, then rub down and respray.

Runs and sagging
Instead of forming a perfectly even coating, the finish runs or sags, sometimes forming a thick roll along one edge of the workpiece. This will occur when the finish is applied too thickly or the finish is overdiluted.
Let the finish dry hard, then rub down with wet-and-dry paper before applying the next coat.

Cissing or fish-eye
A newly sprayed surface develops miniature craters where the finish has been repelled by traces of wax, oil or water. An old piece that has been stripped of its finish may be contaminated by silicone oil or wax from previous finishes. Alternatively, if the compressor receiver or air line has not been drained properly, water or oil may be deposited in the new finish.
When the finish has set, scrape or sand it flat with wet-and-dry paper and wipe the surface clean, using a cloth dampened with white spirit. After draining the spray-gun system, spray a small area to see whether the problem has been eradicated.

If the symptoms recur, rub down again and add a proprietary anti-cissing (fish-eye) agent to the finish to reduce its surface tension.

As a last resort, strip the finish back to bare wood (see pages 31–5) and apply a shellac-based sealer (see page 26) before respraying.

Finish dries with a powdery appearance
A dry, finely textured surface may be the result of excessive air pressure or overspray settling on previously sprayed paintwork. Alternatively, you may be holding the gun so far from the surface that the finish is almost dry when it reaches the surface.
Let the finish dry thoroughly, then rub down and respray.

TYPICAL SPRAY-GUN PROBLEMS
Some faults are caused by not cleaning and servicing a spray gun regularly.

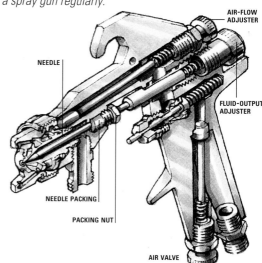

AIR-FLOW ADJUSTER

NEEDLE

FLUID-OUTPUT ADJUSTER

NEEDLE PACKING

PACKING NUT

AIR VALVE

Gun flutters or spits drops
If the gun begins to flutter or spit drops of paint or varnish onto the workpiece while spraying, check to see if the reservoir is nearly empty or the delivery pipe is not in the correct position to pick up the fluid (see page 81). Check also that the air vent in the top of the reservoir has not become blocked. If all seems to be well with the reservoir, try thinning the fluid slightly. Tighten the needle-valve packing nut to ensure it does not allow air into the fluid passages.

Fluid runs from the nozzle
If paint or varnish seeps from the nozzle when the gun is not being operated, the needle packing may be too tight. Lubricate the packing with a spot of light oil and check the adjustment of the packing nut. If this does not solve the problem, the needle itself may be worn or damaged, or may not be seating properly in the fluid tip. Have the gun checked by an expert.

Fluid leaks from the packing nut
Tighten the packing nut; if this does not work, replace the needle packing.

CHAPTER 7

Waxing wood is a long-established tradition, and one which is frequently employed by antique restorers. That is not to say that the subtle qualities of wax polish have gone unnoticed by other woodworkers, especially as a finish for open-grain timbers or as a dressing over lacquer, varnish or French polish.

WAX POLISH

COMMERCIAL POLISHES

Making wax polish from basic ingredients is sometimes advocated by traditionalists, but since there is such a variety of excellent polishes readily available, there seems little point in introducing a complication into what is otherwise one of the simplest of wood-finishing processes. Most commercially prepared wax polishes are a blend of relatively soft beeswax and hard carnauba wax, reduced to a usable consistency with turpentine or white spirit.

A traditional wax finish gives a sympathetic patina to a Georgian-style dressing table and chair

Paste wax polish

The most familiar form of wax polish is sold as a thick paste, packed in flat tins or foil containers. Paste wax, applied with a cloth pad or fine steel wool, serves as an ideal dressing over another finish.

Liquid wax polish

When you want to wax a large area of oak panelling, for example, it is probably easiest to brush on liquid wax polish that has the consistency of cream.

Floor wax

Floor wax is a liquid polish formulated for hardwearing surfaces. It is usually available as a clear polish only.

Tinted brushing polish deepens the colour of pine furniture

Silicones

Silicone oil, which is added to some polishes to make them easier to apply and burnish, will repel most surface coatings should the piece require refinishing in the future (see page 88). Sealing the wood beforehand is a wise precaution, but applying a chemical stripper at a later date may still allow silicone oil to penetrate the pores. You should therefore decide from the beginning whether it would be better to finish a piece with a silicone-free wax polish.

Woodturning sticks

Carnauba wax is the main ingredient for sticks that are hard enough to be used as a friction polish on work-pieces being turned in a lathe.

Coloured polishes

White to pale-yellow polishes do not alter the colour of the wood to a great extent, but there is also an extensive choice of darker shades, sometimes referred to as staining waxes, that can be used to modify the colour of a workpiece and to hide scratches and minor blemishes. Dark-brown to black polish is a popular finish for oak furniture; it enhances the patina of old wood and, by lodging in the open pores, accentuates the grain pattern. There are warm golden-brown polishes, made to put the colour back into stripped pine, and orange-red polishes to enrich faded mahogany. Applying one polish over another creates even more subtle shades and tints.

It is not a good idea to wax chairs or benches with dark-coloured polishes in case your body heat should soften the wax and stain your clothing. The same goes for finishing the insides of drawers; long-term contact could discolour delicate fabrics.

Wax-dressed walnut display cabinet

APPLYING WAX POLISHES

Finishing wood with a wax polish could hardly be simpler, as it requires only careful application and sufficient energy to burnish the surface to a deep shine. However, as with any wood finish, the work-piece must be sanded smooth and any blemishes filled or repaired before you can achieve a satisfactory result (see pages 10–26). Wipe the surface with white spirit (see page 28) to remove traces of grease and old wax polish.

Although there is no need to fill the grain, it is always best to seal the work with two coats of French polish or sanding sealer before applying wax polish, especially if you have coloured the wood with solvent stain. Rub down the sealer coats with fine silicon-carbide paper.

WAX-POLISHING BRUSHES

Professional wood finishers sometimes use a bristle brush to burnish hardened wax polish. You can use a clean shoe brush, but you might want to buy a purpose-made furniture brush fitted with a handle to keep your knuckles out of the way when burnishing into awkward corners and recesses. In addition, there are circular brushes designed to fit the chuck of a power drill; when you are using one of these, apply light pressure only and keep the brush moving across the polished surface.

HAND BRUSH FOR WAX POLISH

DRILL BRUSH

SHOE BRUSH

FURNITURE BRUSH

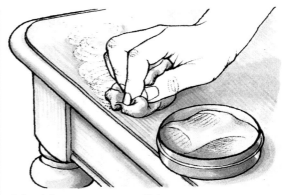

1 Applying paste wax polish
Dip a cloth pad in paste wax and apply the first coat, using overlapping circular strokes to rub the wax into the grain. Cover the surface evenly, then finish by rubbing in the direction of the grain. If the polish proves difficult to spread, warm the tin on a radiator.

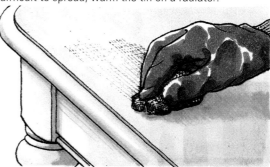

2 Building up a layer of polish
After about 15 to 20 minutes, use 000-grade steel wool or an abrasive nylon pad to rub on more wax polish, this time working along the grain. Put the work aside for 24 hours so that the solvent can evaporate. On new work, apply four or five coats of wax in all, allowing each one to harden overnight.

3 Burnishing the polish
When the wax has hardened thoroughly, burnish vigorously with a soft cloth pad. Some polishers prefer to use a furniture brush because it raises a better shine, particularly when burnishing carved work. Finally, rub over all polished surfaces with a clean duster.

1 Brushing liquid wax polish
Decant some polish into a shallow dish and brush it liberally onto the wood, spreading the wax as evenly as possible. Let the solvent evaporate for about an hour.

2 Applying subsequent coats
Apply a second coat of wax with a soft cloth pad. Use circular strokes at first, and finish by rubbing parallel to the grain. An hour later, apply a third coat if required.

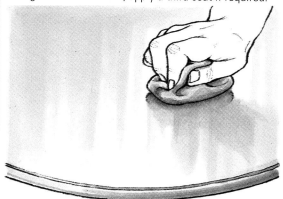

3 Buffing the surface
Leave the polish to harden, preferably overnight, then burnish the workpiece in the direction of the grain with a clean soft duster.

Maintaining a wax finish
The colour and patina of a wax finish improve with age, provided the finish receives regular care. Mop up any spilled water immediately, and dust a polished surface frequently to pick up dirt that might otherwise sink into the wax and discolour the finish. If you cannot raise a satisfactory shine by burnishing with a soft cloth, it is time to apply a fresh coat of wax. Very dowdy wax polish can be removed with white spirit, in preparation for refinishing (see page 28).

APPLYING A WAX DRESSING
If you want to achieve the typical mellow finish of wax polish but prefer something more hardwearing, you can apply a thin wax dressing over polyurethane varnish or cold-cure lacquer.

Dip 000-grade steel wool or an abrasive nylon pad in paste polish, and rub the finished surface using long straight strokes, parallel with the grain. Leave the wax to harden for 15 to 20 minutes, then polish it with a soft cloth.

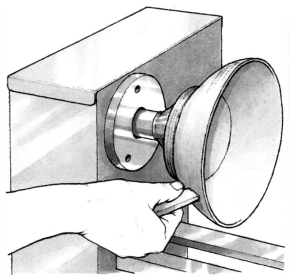

1 Waxing a turned workpiece
Sand the work smooth with fine abrasive paper or cloth, rub a damp cloth along it to raise the grain, then sand the wood a second time when the water has evaporated. Hold a special hard-wax turning stick against the workpiece as it rotates in a lathe at a slow speed – move the stick across the work as friction begins to melt the wax, coating the wood evenly.

You can apply a cloth pad dipped in ordinary paste wax polish to a turned piece, but you may need several coats of wax to build a satisfactory finish.

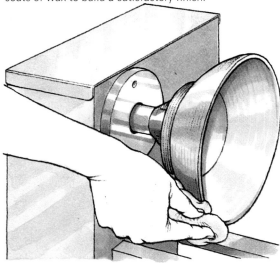

2 Burnishing with the lathe running
Let the wax harden, then hold a soft cloth pad against the rotating workpiece to raise a shine. Move the cloth slowly across the work, keeping the pad away from rotating parts of the lathe. Although you need to apply sufficient pressure to smooth the surface of the wax, pressing too hard can tear the polish.

Polishing floors
After cleaning or sanding wooden floorboards, seal the bare wood with a proprietary floor sealer. Pour clear liquid floor wax into a shallow dish and apply two coats of polish to the wood, using a 100mm (4in) paintbrush. Leave the wax to dry, then burnish the wood with a bristle brush held in a power drill or hire a polishing machine to finish a large floor.

You may need to wax polish a floor every four to six months, depending on the wear it receives; it should be burnished every few weeks to recreate the shine.

FAULTS AND REMEDIES
Wax polishing is so straightforward that there is very little that can go wrong, and even a complete novice can achieve perfect results. Most problems that do occur are caused by impatience.

Uneven finish
Burnishing a polished surface before the solvent has evaporated redistributes the wax, resulting in a patchy, uneven finish. You may also find you are leaving fingerprints in the soft wax.
Leave the wax to harden, then use a 000-grade steel-wool pad to apply a light dressing of fresh wax to even out the finish. Let this coat dry overnight before burnishing with a soft duster.

Surface breaks up when burnishing
The wax has not hardened completely, and rubbing too hard pulls flakes of wax off the surface.
Remove the wax with a steel-wool pad dipped in white spirit. Wipe the dissolved wax off the wood with a paper towel and re-polish.

Wax develops a bloom
Occasionally a wax finish will develop a cloudy bloom as the solvent evaporates.
This effect is usually temporary, and can be removed with a soft duster.

CHAPTER 8

OIL FINISHES

Unlike varnish and paint, which lay on the surface, wood-finishing oil penetrates deeply into the pores, forming a resilient finish that will not crack, peel or chip. As a result, most oil finishes are ideal for exterior joinery and garden furniture, and require no more than annual maintenance to protect the wood from weathering and preserve its appearance.

TYPES OF OIL FINISH

Some woodworkers consider oil finishes as being suitable only for hardwoods such as teak or afrormosia; this is primarily because they are associated in people's minds with the fashion for 'Scandinavian-style' furniture and interior design. In fact, oil makes a handsome finish for any timber, especially pine, which turns a rich golden colour when oiled.

Pine staircase finished with hardwearing gelled oil

Linseed oil

Traditional linseed oil, derived from the flax plant, is rarely used nowadays for finishing wood, mainly because it can take up to three days to dry.

Manufacturers have been able to reduce drying time to about 24 hours by heating the oil and adding driers, producing 'boiled' linseed oil. Neither type of oil should be used as an exterior finish.

Tung oil

Also known as Chinese wood oil, tung oil is obtained from nuts grown in China and parts of South America. A tung-oil finish is resistant to water, alcohol and acidic fruit juice, takes about 24 hours to dry and is suitable for exterior woodwork.

Finishing oil

Commercial wood-finishing oils, based on tung oil, include synthetic resins to improve their durability. Depending on temperature and humidity, finishing oils dry in about six hours. Often referred to as teak oil or Danish oil, finishing oil is an excellent finish for any environment, and can also be used as a sealer coat for oil varnish or paint.

Non-toxic oils

Pure tung oil is non-toxic, but some manufacturers add metallic driers to it, so don't use tung oil for items that will come into contact with food unless the maker's recommendations state specifically that it is safe to do so. As an alternative, you can use ordinary olive oil or one of the special 'salad-bowl' oils, sold for finishing food receptacles and chopping boards.

Gelled oil

A blend of natural oils and synthetic resin is available in a thick gel that behaves more like a soft wax polish. It is packed in tubs so that the gel can be picked up on a cloth pad. Gelled oil can be applied to bare wood and, unlike other oil finishes, it can also be applied over existing finishes such as varnish and lacquer.

Preparing the surface

Since oil is a penetrating finish, it cannot be applied to a pre-varnished or painted workpiece; strip a surface finish using chemical stripper (see pages 31–4). When finishing previously oiled timber, use white spirit to clean old wax from the surface (see page 28). Prepare bare wood thoroughly (see pages 10–26), sanding it smooth with progressively finer abrasive papers.

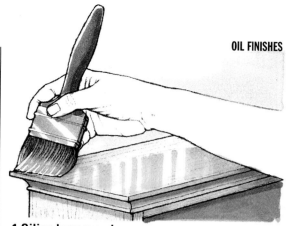

1 Oiling bare wood
Shake the container before decanting some oil into a shallow dish. Apply the first coat, using a fairly wide paintbrush to wet the surface thoroughly. Leave the oil to soak in for about 10 to 15 minutes, then ensure that coverage is even by wiping excess oil from the surface with a soft cloth pad.

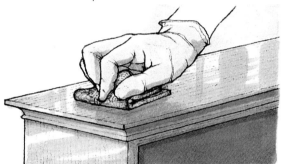

2 Applying additional oil with a pad
After six hours, use an abrasive nylon-fibre pad to rub oil onto the wood in the general direction of the grain. Wipe excess from the surface with a paper towel or cloth pad, then leave it to dry overnight. Apply a third coat in the same way.

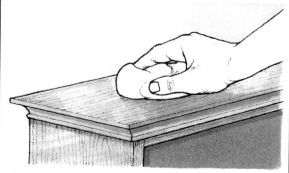

3 Modifying the finish
Leave the last coat to dry thoroughly, then burnish the surface with a duster to raise a soft sheen.

For a smooth satin finish, dress interior woodwork with wax polish, using a clean abrasive nylon pad or fine steel wool (see page 93).

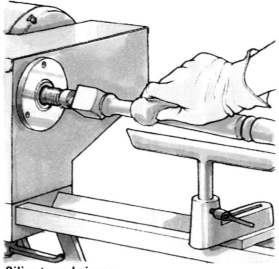

Oiling turned pieces

After sanding a turned workpiece, switch off the lathe while you rub oil onto the wood. Let it soak in for a short while, wipe off excess oil, then restart the lathe and burnish by holding a cloth pad against the slowly rotating workpiece.

Applying gelled oil

Apply gelled oil to bare wood, using a soft cloth pad to rub the finish vigorously in the direction of the grain until the surface is touch-dry. Two coats are usually sufficient, but apply more gelled oil to a workpiece that will be subjected to heavy wear and hot dishes; allow four hours between coats. Apply gelled oil sparingly over an existing finish.

Since gelled oil dries naturally to a soft sheen, there is no need to burnish the workpiece again, but allow a full 48 hours before you put it to use.

From time to time, wipe the workpiece with a damp cloth to remove surface marks and fingerprints.

Maintaining an oiled finish

An oiled surface is very hardwearing, and under normal circumstances requires nothing more than an occasional wipe with a damp cloth to maintain the finish. A faded finish can be revitalised by applying a light coat of oil, provided you remove any wax dressing first (see page 28). Wipe the surface dry before oiling.

Oil exterior woodwork at regular intervals, taking care to treat all surfaces with at least one coat.

Fire precautions

As oil oxidizes it generates heat, which can cause oil-soaked rags to burst into flames. Spread out used rags to dry thoroughly outside, or soak them in a bucket of water overnight before disposing of them.

FAULTS AND REMEDIES

Oiling wood is so easy that success is practically guaranteed, provided you have prepared the work-piece adequately and you don't leave the oil to become sticky.

Sticky surface

If you leave excess oil on the surface for longer than about an hour, it thickens and becomes sticky.
Don't attempt to wipe off oil if it reaches this stage. Instead, use an abrasive nylon pad to apply a light dressing of fresh oil to wet the surface again, then wipe over with a cloth pad or absorbent paper towel.

White rings

Hot plates or dishes may leave white rings on an oiled surface.
These blemishes are usually temporary and disappear of their own accord within a short time.

CHAPTER 9

Covering wood with genuine gold leaf is a particularly skilful process, and is best left to an expert. However, applying paper-thin sheets of gold-coloured base metal is far less demanding and relatively inexpensive. And if you want to spruce up old picture frames and mirrors, you may be able to achieve the desired result with a ready-to-use gilt cream or varnish.

GILDING WITH CREAMS AND VARNISHES

Gilding does not have to be an expensive process. If all you require is an attractive gold-coloured surface, you can use proprietary finishes that are akin to wax polishes and metallic varnishes. Similar products are perfect for improving the appearance of cheap gilded photo mounts and picture frames.

FONTENAY BASE

GILT VARNISH

GILT CREAM

GILT-FINISHING LIQUID

Gilt cream
Soft creamy wax is ready-made in a variety of metallic shades for finishing new work or restoring old gilded furniture and frames. Gilt creams are very easy to apply and mix on the surface of a workpiece.

Gilt varnish
Use non-tarnishing gilt varnish to decorate both new and stripped workpieces. You can apply it directly to the wood or over a traditional red base (see below), and it can be used as a base coat for gilt cream. Gilt varnish is especially useful for picking out small areas of a decorative frame or for finishing separate slip mouldings. Stir gilt varnish thoroughly to avoid a streaky finish.

Fontenay base
Before applying a gilt finish, you can seal the wood with Fontenay base, a special dark-red matt varnish that adds depth to the gold colour. A black base coat, that creates an undertone for silver and pewter finishes, is also available.

Gilt-finishing liquid
Gilt-finish suppliers provide a clear gloss copal varnish for sealing gilt cream. Apply gilt-finishing liquid with a soft paintbrush.

APPLYING FONTENAY BASE
When gilding new work, fill the grain (see page 26) and sand the wood carefully. Rub down paintwork with wet-and-dry paper.

Brush Fontenay base onto the work, leave it to dry, then rub down with very fine steel wool or silicon-carbide paper. If necessary, apply a second base coat to create an even matt finish.

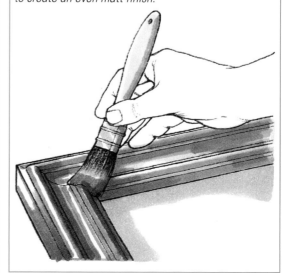

1 Applying gilt cream
Apply gilt cream with a soft cloth wrapped round a fingertip. Use small overlapping circular strokes to spread the cream evenly, finishing with straight parallel strokes. Work cream into carvings and decorative mouldings with an old toothbrush.

2 Burnishing and sealing gilt cream
Allow the solvent to evaporate for at least 12 hours, then burnish the gilded surface with a soft cloth pad. Unless you want an aged appearance, take care not to rub so hard that you expose the base coat on the high points. Apply extra cream to cover any bare patches.

Gilt cream provides a permanent finish similar to ordinary wax polish; for additional protection, coat it with gilt-finishing liquid.

Applying gilt varnish to new work
Using a soft paintbrush, apply gilt varnish evenly and leave it to dry for at least three hours before handling the workpiece. For an extra-rich finish, rub on a darker gilt cream after the varnish has set.

AGEING A GILT FINISH
Good-quality metallic varnishes and creams provide a beautiful finish with a deep glow, but period-style furniture and genuine old pieces often benefit from a little 'ageing' to provide them with a distinguished, care-worn appearance.

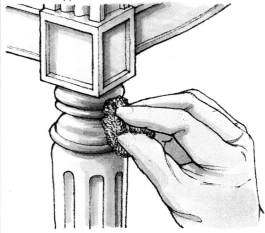

Exposing the basecoat
Using a small ball of fine steel wool or an abrasive nylon-fibre pad, gently rub the gilding from the high points until the red base coat just begins to show through the gold. Take care to keep the treatment subtle, or the effect will be spoiled.

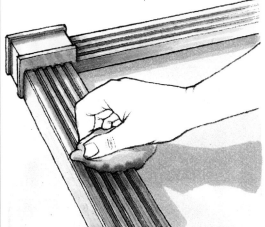

Applying coloured wax
Rub dark-brown wax polish over a newly gilded workpiece, if necessary using a brush to stipple the polish into all the crevices. Take a soft cloth and rub excess wax from the high points, leaving the darker colour to accentuate the decorative details. Create a similar effect by rubbing one or more dark-gold creams over a pale gilt finish, then polish the high spots with a cloth pad.

MAKING MINOR REPAIRS WITH GILDING WAX

It generally pays to exercise restraint when restoring old gilding. Even run-of-the-mill picture frames become more characterful when natural wear starts to expose the dark base colour and the gilding begins to take on a mellowed patina. The best policy is to patch up only those faults that draw attention to themselves, disguising them with a blend of wax sticks and gilt cream.

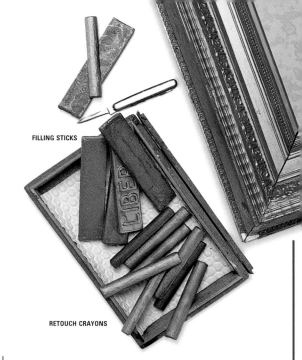

FILLING STICKS

RETOUCH CRAYONS

Disguising open mitres
You can fill a less-than-perfect mitre joint with a soft wax crayon. Rub the sharp edge of the stick across the open mitre until it is filled flush with wax. Wrap a soft cloth around your finger, and rub along the joint to smooth the filling and remove excess wax from the surface. If necessary, blend the colour with a fingertip dipped in gilt cream.

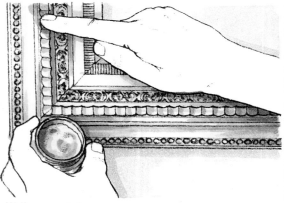

Hiding scratches
Fill a deep scratch that has exposed the red base colour or white gesso ground (see page 104) with a soft wax crayon (see above), and hide minor scratches by rubbing over them with gilt cream.

Wax filling sticks and retouch crayons
Use gilt-coloured wax sticks to fill holes and repair minor chips and damaged mouldings. Softer-wax crayons will help disguise scratches and inaccurate mitre joints. Both types of wax stick are available in a wide range of colours and tones, from deep bronze to pale gold and silver. Melting two or more sticks and blending the wax allows you to match an existing finish exactly.

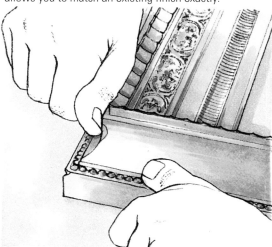

Filling holes
When restoring an old picture frame, fill small holes with a gilt filling stick of hard wax. Soften a pea-size piece of wax on a radiator until you can knead it easily between your fingers, then use a penknife to press the softened wax into each hole. Scrape it level with your thumbnail or a plastic credit card, and burnish the wax filling with the smooth paper backing of abrasive paper. Disguise the repair by smearing it with gilt cream.

GILDING WITH METAL LEAF

Base-metal leaf is not a cheap modern substitute for genuine gold leaf. For hundreds of years it has been employed for work that did not merit the expense of being coated with pure gold, so metal leaf can be used legitimately to make attractive repairs as well as for gilding new work

Gilded sconce (right)
Flickering candlelight will accentuate the quality of genuine gold leaf or base-metal gilding.

Empire-style couch (below)
The appeal of this elegant couch is greatly enhanced by its ebonized frame with gilded details.

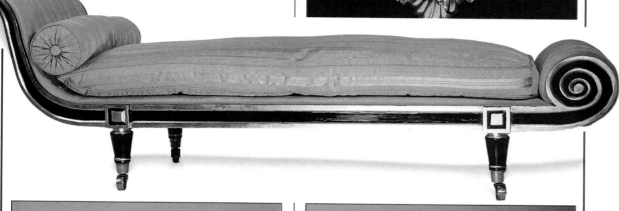

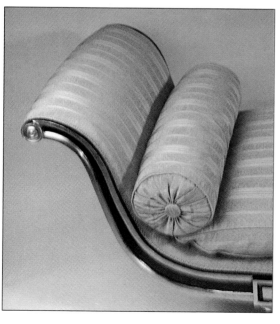

GOLD SIZE

BOLE

METAL
LACQUER

METAL LEAF

Metal leaf

Also known as common leaf or Dutch leaf, metal leaf, an alloy of copper and zinc, is available as thin 100 to 125mm (4 to 5in) squares bound into books of 25 sheets. Being slightly thicker than gold leaf, metal leaf is relatively easy to apply and, when burnished, makes a passable substitute for the real thing.

Gesso and bole

Far from hiding uneven grain or surface blemishes, thin metal leaf will highlight imperfections as soon as it is burnished. Consequently, bare wood is coated with gesso, a paste made from rabbit-skin glue and chalk, which can be sanded to a perfectly smooth base for gilding. It can also be used as a glue for re-attaching broken pieces of old gesso. Coloured gesso is sometimes referred to as bole.

Gold size

Size is a glue-like preparation used to stick metal leaf to a gesso ground. Depending on the type you use, size will dry in anything from 2 to 24 hours.

Metal lacquer

Base metal will tarnish unless it is coated with a water-clear transparent lacquer formulated to protect metal.

PREPARING METAL LEAF

Before you handle metal leaf, wash your hands and dust them with talcum powder to prevent the leaf sticking to your fingers.

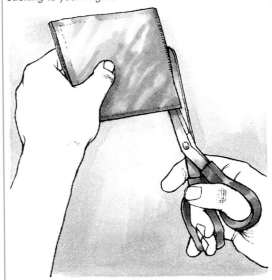

Cutting the leaves to size
Remove the outer covers from a book of metal leaf and cut off the spine with scissors. Leaving the tissue backing intact, trim each individual sheet into squares or rectangles to fit the work in progress.

Preparing the surface
Fill any holes and cracks, then sand the wood as smooth as possible. Wipe the surface with white spirit to remove dust and grease.

1 Applying bole to the work

Warm a pot of ready-made dark-red bole in a *bain-marie* or glue pot until it becomes liquid enough to be brushed smoothly onto the prepared surface. Don't allow the bole to run or collect in the hollows.

Leave the surface to harden overnight, then rub it down lightly with fine wet-and-dry paper. Apply up to five coats of bole.

4 Sizing the workpiece

Apply a thin, even coat of adhesive gold size, brushing it out carefully to avoid leaving bare patches. Since metal leaf must be applied to the size at exactly the right moment, divide a large workpiece into smaller, manageable sections.

2 Sealing the bole with shellac

Mix up a sealer comprising equal amounts of standard French polish and methylated spirit. Apply the thinned shellac with a cloth pad or a soft paintbrush; when brushing up to sharp edges or mouldings, take care that the sealer does not run or collect in grooves or hollows.

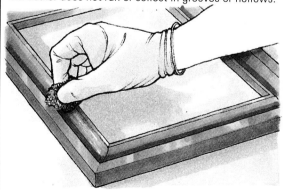

5 Testing the size

Temperature and humidity will affect the time it takes for gold size to dry. Check by gently touching your knuckles against the sized surface; when it feels firm but slightly tacky, the size is about ready.

3 Rubbing down with steel wool

Allow the shellac to harden, then remove blemishes by rubbing down gently with 0000-grade steel wool lubricated with soapy water. Wipe the surface dry with a clean cloth.

6 Applying metal leaf

Holding a leaf of metal in both hands, lay it face-down onto the sized workpiece. Smooth it down firmly with your fingertips, then peel off the tissue backing.

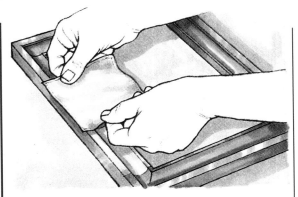

7 Overlapping each leaf
Apply the next strip of metal leaf in the same way, overlapping its neighbour by about 3mm (⅛in). Continue to lay additional strips until you have gilded the entire workpiece, or at least one sized section.

8 Blending the joints
Remove the overlaps and blend the joints between strips of leaf by brushing them with the tip of an ox-hair paintbrush. Brush only in the direction of the overlaps, collecting the tiny scraps of leaf on a piece of paper placed beneath the workpiece. These 'skewings' are used to patch small areas at the next stage.

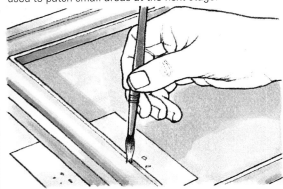

9 Patching with skewings
Inspect the work carefully for areas of red ground that may have been missed. Anything that is too small to be covered with a small patch of metal leaf can be obliterated with skewings brushed lightly onto the surface and tamped down firmly onto the still-tacky size with the tip of a brush.

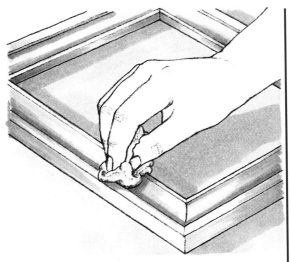

10 Burnishing the leaf
The following day, burnish the metal gently with a cotton-wool pad until you have raised a soft sheen. Preserve the finish by brushing the workpiece with a thin coat of transparent metal lacquer.

GILDING CARVED WORK
Gilding a carved workpiece takes more time and patience. Consequently, plan to size and gild sections in turn, so that you can apply leaf to one part of the work while the size is becoming tacky on another. This may entail working from the bottom up, to avoid skewings contaminating a section that is still drying.

Applying leaf to shaped groundwork
Cut or tear small pieces of leaf to fit the shape of the area you are working on, pressing them into place with your fingertips until you have completed a section, then tamp the metal with the tip of a brush to ensure it conforms to the shape of the groundwork and adheres to the size.

CHAPTER 10

Graining is the art of simulating the appearance of real wood with coloured glaze. Although it would be unrealistic to expect to copy actual species of timber without expert tuition, the techniques covered in this chapter will enable you to paint convincing wood effects, using easily available materials and a minimum of specialized brushes and tools.

WOOD GRAINING

GRAINING TOOLS

You can use household-decorating tools to make a reasonable attempt at straightforward graining, but better results and a wider range of subtleties can be achieved if you also invest in a few specialized graining tools.

Professional graining brushes are not cheap, but you should never have to replace them, provided they are kept clean and stored carefully.

A set of metal combs is also relatively expensive, but you can get similar effects from cheaper rubber or plastic combs; you can also cut your own from plastic sheet or cardboard.

You may be able to buy some graining tools from a good general paint stockist, but you will probably have to seek out a specialist tool store or craft supplier to get the full range.

Brushes
Use ordinary decorator's paintbrushes to apply glaze and create simple wood graining. Good-quality brushes are always best for general-purpose work, but cheap or worn paintbrushes may prove to be invaluable for special one-off dragged effects (see page 112–13).

1 Mottler
A mottler, with its short soft bristles, is used to simulate the bands of highlights that are often displayed across wavy-grain woods and veneers, such as fiddleback sycamore or ripple ash. Although a genuine mottler is a useful tool to have in your kit, you can produce similar effects with an ordinary paintbrush.

2 Lining tool
This paintbrush, with its square-trimmed filling of bristles, is ideal for removing excess colour that has accumulated around the edges of a panel or down the sides of dragged grain. However, you can perform similar tasks using any convenient brush.

3 Softener
A 100mm (4in) hog-hair softener is the one specialist brush you cannot do without. The application of a softener spreads and blends marks left by other brushes and tools, turning them into delightful impressions of real wood grain.

4 Flogger
A flogger has extra-long stiff bristles that are used to strike wet glaze, leaving a texture that realistically simulates large open pores. Although you will not use a flogger for every job, it is difficult to achieve the same results with any other brush.

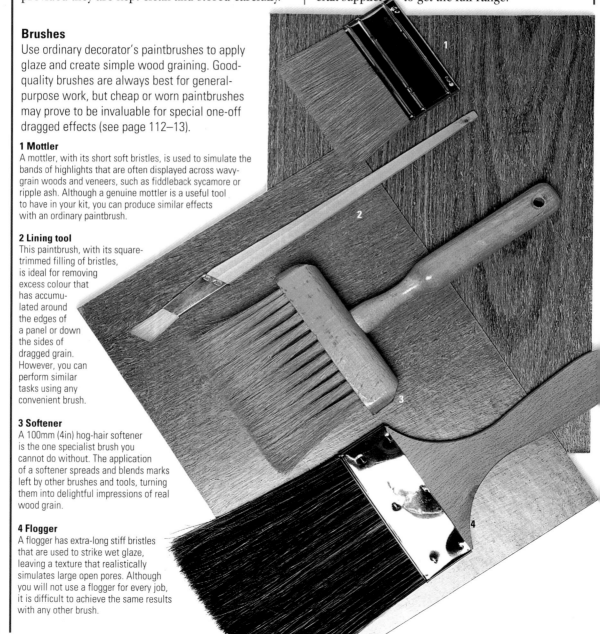

Combs and heart grainers

Dragging the teeth of ready-made or improvised combs through wet glaze leaves a pattern of stripes that is strongly reminiscent of wood grain.

1 Heart grainers
These are special combing tools that leave a highly realistic impression of heart-wood grain. The convex working surface of each heart grainer is moulded with raised concentric ridges, centred on one edge of the tool. A handle is moulded onto the back. Heart grainers are made in coarse, medium and fine grades.

2 Improvised combs
Many wood grainers make their own combs, using thick cardboard or stiff plastic sheet. Cut rectangles or triangles with perfectly flat sides then, using a sharp craft knife, cut a series of deep notches to form the teeth. Depending on the effect you want to create, cut a row of identical teeth or space them irregularly. You can also experiment with ready-made tile-adhesive spreaders.

3 Rubber or plastic combs
Rubber or plastic graining combs, which often have different-size teeth on each edge, produce relatively large striations in the coloured glaze.

4 Steel combs
You can buy sets of precision-made steel combs in three grades – coarse, medium and fine. Combs 75 to 100mm (3 to 4in) wide are the most useful, but you will find 25 and 50mm (1 and 2in) combs perfect for graining narrow rails and stiles.

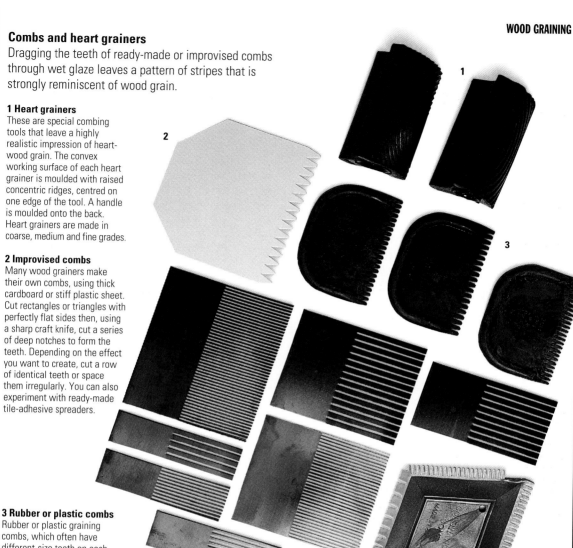

CHECK ROLLER

This very specialized roller is made up of a number of serrated steel discs mounted side-by-side on a central spindle. Its sole function is to print a representation of the deep elongated pores found on open-grain woods, especially oak. Although a check roller is not an essential item, it would be very laborious to create a similar effect by other means.

109

PAINTS AND GLAZES

Standard solvent-based eggshell paint is used to provide the background colour for wood-grain effects. The paint is applied to prepared solid wood or a groundwork cut from man-made board.

Choose a paint that matches the lightest colour in the grain pattern of the wood being simulated; this invariably is found within a limited range of colours, often a pale beige which you may want to tint to a warmer or cooler shade. Accurate colour matching comes with experience and the knowledge of how a background colour is affected when it is overlaid with different glazes. It pays to develop your sense of colour by practising on sheets of stiff card.

Oil glaze
Glaze is a ready-made, practically colourless finish, similar in consistency to conventional paint. However, unlike paint, which is designed to form a flat even covering, oil glaze or 'scumble' is formulated to retain brushstrokes and the marks left by dragging combs across a wet surface.

Artist's oil paints
You can buy wood-coloured glazes, but you will have greater control over the tones and shades of your work if you tint colourless glaze with tubes of oil paint, sold by art-material stockists. The best-quality paints are expensive, but you can use cheaper student-quality oil paints. Earth colours – such as raw and burnt umber, raw and burnt sienna and Vandyke brown – are the most useful for wood graining. You will also need a tube of black paint to alter the tone of the colours where appropriate.

Varnish
After the initial work has dried thoroughly, protect finished wood graining with one or two coats of satin-finish oil varnish (see pages 68–71). You can include mottling in the first coat of varnish (see page 119).

Preparing surfaces
New wood must be sound, clean and dry. After sanding the surface smooth, treat resinous knots with shellac-based knotting (see page 51) before applying a primer and undercoat.

Sand previously finished wood to create a good key for the background colour. Scrape and sand peeling paintwork back to sound feathered edges. Prime bare patches, then obliterate the old colour with a suitable undercoat (see page 76).

When the undercoat is dry, brush or spray the work with two coats of eggshell paint, rubbing down with wet-and-dry paper between applications.

OIL GLAZE

ARTIST'S OIL PAINTS

VARNISH

Applying glaze to groundwork

Whatever your intended final effect, apply the coloured glaze the same way, brushing in all directions to cover the work. You can include irregular streaks of colour by occasionally wiping the brush across the open end of an oil-paint tube and blending the neat paint into the applied glaze. Finish by brushing roughly parallel to the direction of the grain pattern.

The glaze will be perfect for tooling after about five minutes, and will remain workable for up to an hour. When graining a large area, apply the glaze to small, self-contained sections.

EGGSHELL PAINT

MIXING GLAZE

Professionals frequently carry out wood graining with watercolour glazes, but an oil glaze is easier for amateurs to handle, because it leaves plenty of time to create the desired effects. Oil glaze, which is thinned to a usable consistency with white spirit, can be purchased from craft shops or trade suppliers.

Diluting oil paint

Squeeze a 50mm (2in) length of oil paint onto an old saucer, and use a paintbrush to blend in enough white spirit to make the paint very slightly liquid. Blend in other oil-paint colours until you have mixed the shade you want.

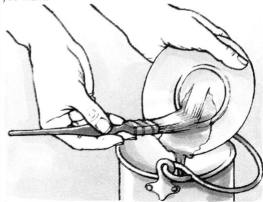

Colouring the glaze

Pour some colourless glaze into a paint kettle – 25mm (1in) of glaze in a 1 litre (2 pint) kettle will be enough for the average room door. Add about 20 per cent white spirit and mix it in thoroughly, then gradually add the thinned oil paint until the glaze appears to be the required colour and consistency. If you add too much white spirit, the glaze may not adhere properly and may dry before you complete the work. If you don't add enough, ridges will form in the glaze as it sets.

Test the glaze by brushing it onto a small area of the prepared work – it should appear darker than the painted groundwork but should retain brushmarks, allowing the base colour to show through.

BRUSH-GRAINING

Before attempting to paint an impression of wood grain, it is essential to examine a few examples of the real thing, in order to get some idea of what different grain patterns look like. This contributes immeasurably to a convincing representation. However, no two pieces of wood are exactly the same, so be prepared to accept the happy accidents that are bound to occur, rather than risk becoming frustrated by striving for a slavish copy.

One of the most immediate techniques is simple brush-graining, which recreates the true character of straight-grained wood.

Graining with a wet paintbrush

Using a wet brush

You can produce muted linear effects by graining with a brush that is still wet from the glaze previously applied to the work. Holding the paintbrush lightly between your thumb and fingertips, drag it from top to bottom at a shallow angle to the work surface, allowing the bristles to disperse the coloured glaze naturally. There is no need to apply excessive pressure, but keep the brush moving throughout the stroke. Apply successive strokes alongside until you have covered the working area.

Using a dry brush

Brush-graining with a dry brush not only displaces the glaze but also removes some colour at the same time, creating relatively bold stripes. Don't be afraid to wobble the brush slightly as you make the strokes, because this adds to the naturalistic appearance, but be sure to follow any diversions when you make successive strokes. Regularly wipe the tips of the bristles onto an absorbent rag to remove excess glaze.

Experiment with different brushes to see what effects they produce; ordinary decorator's paintbrushes, hog-hair softeners, floggers, and even old glue brushes will leave distinctive tracks in the glaze.

A dry brush creates a relatively bold linear texture

Softening the grain

If brush-graining appears too strident, use a softener to blur the lines. Softening also introduces attractive and convincing random factors to the work. Hold the brush at 90 degrees to the surface, and gently stroke the bristles along the painted grain, reducing its intensity without entirely losing the linear effect. Softening across the grain is faster, but you may lose the linear effect altogether.

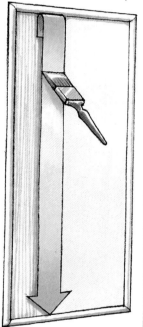

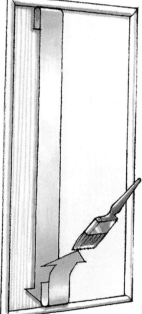

Brush-graining a door panel

Brush-graining panels surrounded by rails, stiles or muntins requires a slight variation in technique.

First paint coloured glaze over the entire panel, then start each graining stroke by pushing the tips of the bristles up against the underside of the top rail and dragging the brush to the bottom.

Reverse the paintbrush and push the bristles down to meet the bottom rail, then draw the brush upwards to meet the initial stroke, lifting it off the surface in one continuous movement. Disguise a poor match by softening the grain (see top right) or texturing the panel with a flogger (see right).

FLOGGING OPEN-GRAIN TEXTURE

Superimpose a coarse open-grain texture over bold linear grain or painted heartwood (see page 114-15).

Using the flogger

Hold the flogger just above and parallel to the surface. Working up from the base of the panel, strike the wet glaze with a series of short over-lapping strokes, using the flat of the brush, until you gradually texture the whole area. To blend the texture near the bottom of the panel, reverse the brush as described left. Use the edge of the brush on narrow workpieces.

PAINTING HEARTWOOD

Wall panelling and frame-and-panel doors are greatly enhanced by the inclusion of bold grain patterns. Mature wood, found near the centre of a tree, produces various irregular grain patterns, depending on how the tree is converted to boards or veneers. The techniques described here simulate a typical pattern of concentric heartwood grain, as found on crown-cut veneer, with straight-grained wood on each side.

For a relatively soft, muted effect, paint the grain pattern onto a background already wet with coloured glaze. For greater contrast, perhaps for work that will be seen from a distance, paint the grain with coloured glaze onto dry groundwork or onto a background that has been 'oiled-in' sparingly with colourless glaze applied with a rag.

Highly figured panels usually appear most attractive when the surrounding stiles and rails are finished with simple brush-graining.

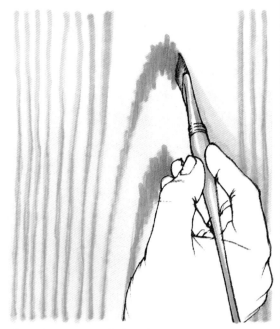

1 Painting concentric bands
Starting from the base of the panel, use an artist's flat fitch to paint concentric bands of coloured glaze. Use the thin edge of the brush for the vertical strokes, painting the pointed apex of each band with the wider face of the brush. You can afford to be quite bold at this stage.

Painting onto dry ground
When the groundwork is left unglazed, more of the pale background colour is exposed and the edges of the heartwood banding remain distinct, even after they have been softened or flogged.

2 Softening the grain pattern
Stroke the softener vertically along the centre of the grain pattern, streaking the pointed tip of each band of colour, then brush to the left and right at an angle of about 30 degrees from the centre. Finish with light vertical strokes.

3 Brush-graining on each side of the banding
Cover the panel on each side of the grain pattern with coloured glaze, then drag the bristles of a paintbrush or softener through the glaze (see pages 112–13), following the general direction of the banding. Soften this brush-graining.

GRAINING RAILS AND STILES
Work to a sequence that allows you to grain up to the joints between rails, stiles and muntins without obliterating the work you have just completed.

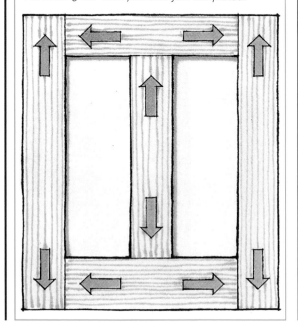

Painting onto wet glaze
When you paint onto groundwork wet with glaze, there is inevitably less contrast between the simulated grain and background colour. If required, you can compensate by mixing a slightly darker glaze for painting the grain.

Begin by applying coloured glaze to the entire background, then brush-grain roughly with the wet paintbrush (see page 112). Take some of the coloured glaze and add more oil paint to darken the tone, thinning it slightly with white spirit.

Paint and soften heartwood banding (see opposite), then complete the panel with brush-graining on each side of the central grain pattern.

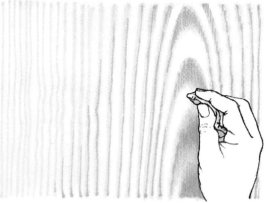

Blotting highlights
If, having softened the work, you require more contrast between grain pattern and background, fold an absorbent rag into a pad and use one edge to blot some of the glaze from between the bands of colour. Lightly soften or flog the work.

COMB-GRAINING

When done well, combing is highly evocative of coarse open-grain wood, and sometimes exhibits attractive interference patterns that are similar in appearance to silky oak. The basic techniques are not difficult to master, and with practice you will discover the degree of variation required to avoid an over-repetitive, mechanical effect. Combing is employed primarily to produce the near-parallel linear patterns of straight-grained wood, but you can use steel or rubber combs to blur painted or dragged oak heartwood and to break up coarse brush-graining.

When combing, it pays to add a little more white spirit to the glaze, to avoid ridges building up where the comb's teeth push the glaze aside.

Oak grain pattern created with steel combs

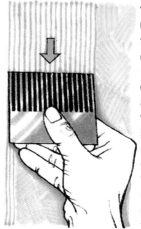

1 Using steel combs
Cover the surface with thinned glaze and brush it out well, then draw a 100mm (4in) medium steel comb from top to bottom in a series of overlapping vertical strokes. Keep the strokes more-or-less parallel, but imitate real grain by allowing the comb to waver from side to side occasionally. Wipe excess glaze from the tips of the teeth between strokes.

2 Reverse combing
Break up the linear pattern with a fine comb, dragging it upwards at an angle of about 10 degrees to the first series of strokes. Blend in excess colour at the top and bottom of a panel by stippling with a lining tool. Go back over the same area a second time if you want to create a finer texture, or blur parts of the work by stippling gently with a softener.

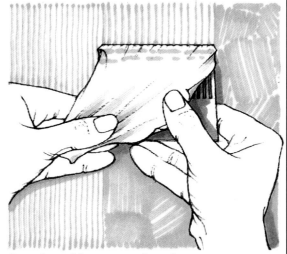

Dragging with a wrapped comb
To create a relatively subdued effect, wrap a piece of absorbent rag tightly over the teeth of a coarse or medium comb. Drag the wrapped comb through the glaze, pulling a clean section of the rag over the tips of the teeth after each vertical stroke. Cover the work-piece once, and then break up the pattern with an unwrapped fine comb, as described left.

USING A HEART GRAINER

A heart grainer is employed exclusively to simulate the pattern of dense heartwood grain. It is used much like a comb, in that it is drawn across the work to leave impressions in the wet glaze, but by presenting its convex surface to the work at different angles, you can create an almost infinite variety of bold patterns with a single tool.

Rubber grainers are moulded with coarse, medium or fine ribs – a coarse grade is ideal for oak heartwood, whereas the finer grades are more reminiscent of pine.

Holding a heart grainer
Hold the grainer between thumb and fingertips, with the concentric curved ribs centred on the bottom edge of the tool.

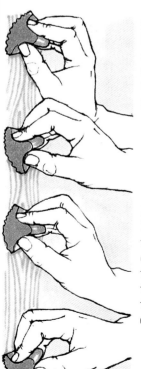

Starting the stroke
Position the grainer near one end of the workpiece, with the bottom edge of the tool resting on the glazed surface.

Making the stroke
Draw the grainer slowly to the bottom of the panel in one continuous stroke, at the same time rocking the tool over and back to vary the pattern left in the coloured glaze.

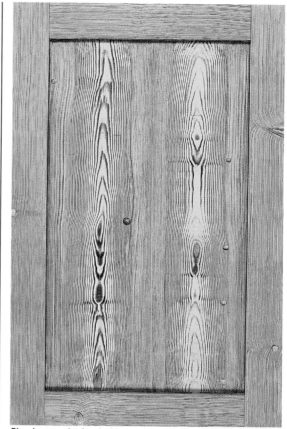

Pine door panel painted with a heart grainer and dry brush

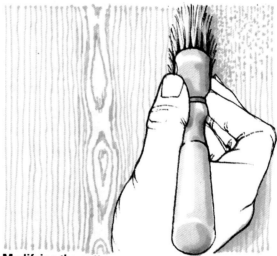

Modifying the pattern
Create a suggestion of straight grain on each side of the heartwood pattern, following its outline roughly with a brush or comb, then soften and blend both grain patterns (see pages 114–15). Alternatively, you can modify the work with light flogging, or retain better definition by stippling with a softener.

ADDITIONAL FIGURING

Small details applied to basic brush- or comb-graining add variety and interest, making each panel or frame a unique piece of work. Such detailing must be done with care to be convincing, but this does not mean that its application has to be laboured; a degree of spontaneity is vital in producing lively work. One essential requirement is a familiarity with the effects you are trying to create; this can best be achieved by collecting examples of real wood or accurate colour reproductions from which to work.

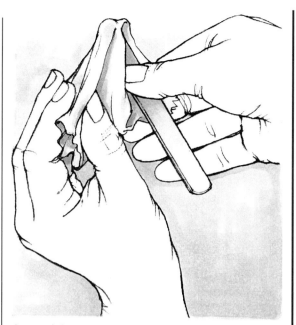

Improvising a veining horn
Professional grainers use a flat pointed tool, known as a veining horn, wrapped in absorbent cloth for wiping out ray flecks. Some grainers improvise by wrapping a coin, but a simple wooden spatula or ice-cream stick is easier to handle. Stretch the fabric tightly over the rounded tip of the stick, re-folding the rag at intervals to maintain a clean working edge.

Creating quartered oak
Quarter-sawing logs reveals a grain pattern crossed with ray-fleck figure in some hardwoods, especially oak. These pale-coloured flecks can be found running ribbon-like down a piece of straight-grained wood, or perhaps flanking a central band of bold figure.

Reproduce ray flecks by wiping them out of combed or brushed-and-flogged graining.

Wiping out individual flecks
Draw the cloth-covered tool through the glaze, turning the stick to make short twisting lines that taper sharply towards their ends. No two flecks are identical in shape or size, but they tend to follow a similar pattern across the work.

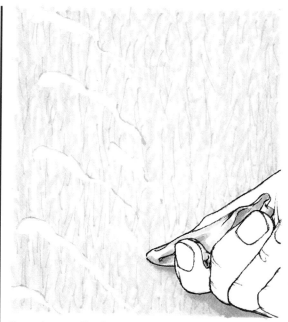

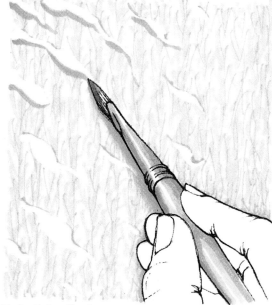

Grouping ray flecks
Wipe out staggered rows of ray flecks, making them smaller and fainter as you approach the edge of a panel. Lightly soften the work with a brush or comb, but take care not to lose too much definition.

Underlining flecks
When the work is to be seen from a distance, you can create depth and variety by underlining some ray flecks with dark glaze. Use an artist's fitch to apply the glaze freely, then soften the marks or blend them with light stippling.

Mottling
There are several ways to produce the silky mottle of reflective grain pattern exhibited by hardwoods such as mahogany and satinwood, but perhaps the easiest method is to create the effect when applying the final protective coats of varnish. Darken the varnish with slightly thinned oil paint, then brush it evenly onto the workpiece. Because oil varnish dries faster than glaze, you may find it necessary to mottle a large workpiece in manageable stages.

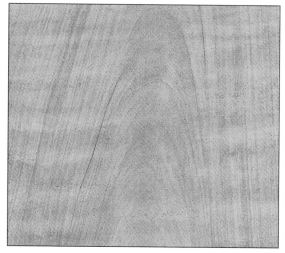

Mottled satinwood

Using a mottler
Holding the mottler at 45 degrees to the surface, remove narrow strips of varnish by waggling the brush from side to side. Create a band of separate, slightly random, impressions in the varnish. Keep the bristles dry by wiping them on an absorbent rag.

Mottling with a paintbrush
Squeeze the bristles of a household paintbrush between your fingers and thumb to produce a narrow, slightly wavy tip. To soften mottling, gently stroke the bristles of a softener along the impressions – never across them.

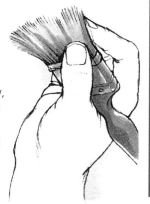

Including knots

Knots can be found in practically any species of timber, but they are particularly prevalent in softwoods. It can enliven grain patterns if you include the occasional knot when painting.

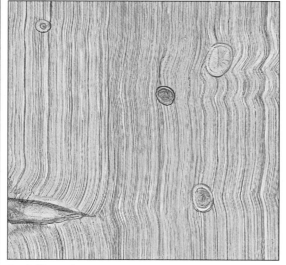

Detail of knotty pine

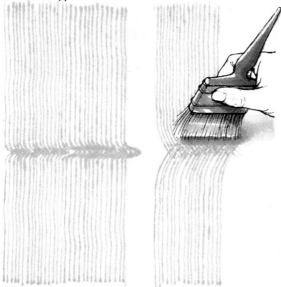

Placing knots

You can place a small knot almost anywhere that would benefit from some additional interest, but for special emphasis consider the placing of knots while applying the initial graining. For example, while drawing a brush through wet glaze, make a sharp kink to one side; a knot would nestle realistically in the bend.

Alternatively, manufacture some wild grain by flicking the brush to one side in the down stroke, then draw the brush up from the base of the work, flicking the brush in the same direction where the strokes meet.

Imprinting knots

It is surprisingly easy to imprint a realistic knot in wet glaze, using the end of a dowel or even your fingertip if you are wearing protective gloves. The simple act of touching the glaze disperses the colour, leaving a pale patch with a darker rim and sometimes a small dark dot in the centre.

If a knot needs still further emphasis, paint in small concentric circles very freely with the point of an artist's brush, stippling afterwards to soften the effect. Don't make all the knots the same shape or size.

PRINTING DEEP PORES

Some cuts of oak, walnut and, to a lesser extent, beech, exhibit deep, elongated pores. These can be printed over brushed or combed grain once the initial work is dry, using a check roller.

Using a check roller

Apply a dark-coloured glaze with a paintbrush held against the serrated discs of a check roller as you push the tool across the work. The pores should run at a very slight angle across the general direction of the grain.

CHAPTER 11 The patina of old woodwork – greatly admired and respected by restorers and collectors – is acquired naturally by long exposure to light, the gradual accumulation of dust and grease, and by moderate wear and tear. Although it is not that easy to reproduce the subtleties of a genuine patina, you can give both new and older pieces an attractive aged appearance by gently 'distressing' their finishes.

ANTIQUE FINISHES

SHADING A CLEAR FINISH

Shading is a technique that reproduces the modulations of colour and tone found on old polished or varnished items. The parts of a piece that are handled regularly or that receive the most wear are generally paler than those areas that are protected. Similarly, large flat areas, which are polished and dusted regularly, are cleaner than corners and crevices where dirt is able to collect.

Shading suggests the accumulation of dirt and old polish

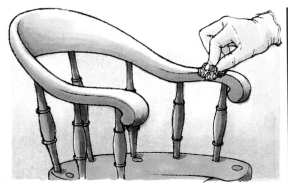

2 Removing colour
When the stain is dry, use a pad of fine steel wool to remove some of the colour. Concentrate on those areas that would have been rubbed and handled regularly, such as chair backs, seats and arms, and suggest a degree of wear on stretcher rails. Similarly, lightly scuff mouldings, carvings and edges to remove colour from the high points.

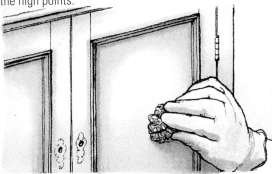

3 Shading door panels
Create a pale patch in the centre of a door panel, with a gradual transition from light to dark towards the perimeter of the panel. Rub in the direction of the grain only, avoiding sudden changes of tone.

4 Finishing touches
Carefully wipe the surfaces with a cloth dampened with solvent to remove dust and particles of metal.

If required, accentuate mouldings and carving by brushing tinted French polish into the deeper crevices (see page 48). Finish the workpiece with a dark-brown paste wax polish, emphasizing the gradual changes of colour and tone that you have created.

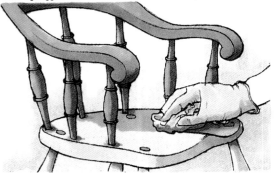

1 Applying stain
Prepare the workpiece, sanding it smooth, then apply a penetrating wood stain (see pages 42–6). Because you will be removing much of the colour in the next stage of the process, use a stain that is darker than you would normally choose for colouring similar pieces.

DISTRESSING PAINTWORK

A perfectly finished item may look incongruous in a country setting or when placed among older, weathered pieces. Give new paintwork a suitably well-used patina with coloured wax polishes or a wash coat of tinted oil glaze. Finish the workpiece with matt or eggshell paint. There is no need to strive for a perfect finish; ageing processes work best with slightly uneven paintwork.

Paintwork distressed with coloured wax polish

1 Applying coloured wax polish

When the paint is dry, use an abrasive nylon pad to apply coloured paste wax polish to the entire workpiece. Rub in all directions to encourage wax to lodge in the recesses, including scratches and other imperfections. Take care not to wear through the paint at this stage. Applying two different colours to vary the overall tone makes for an interesting effect.

2 Modifying the colour

Leave the coloured wax to dry, then use a clean abrasive pad dipped in colourless wax polish to clean the dark colour from the surfaces, especially the high points. Be sure to remove most of the colour from the central areas of flat panels, leaving more of the dark polish where dirt would collect naturally. Don't worry if you happen to wear through the paintwork on a few high points and edges – it only adds to the overall effect.

Remove excess wax with a soft cloth and, the next day, burnish to a soft sheen.

DISTRESSING WITH OIL GLAZE

As an alternative to wax polish, distress new paintwork with oil glaze tinted to the required colour with artist's oil paint (see page 111). Allow the base coat of eggshell paint to dry, then brush the tinted glaze freely across all surfaces.

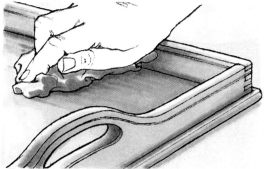

Removing coloured glaze

After about five minutes, wipe off most of the glaze with a pad of soft absorbent cloth, leaving the residue to settle in the recesses and deeper blemishes. If the effect is not to your liking, you have plenty of time to wash off the glaze with a cloth dampened with white spirit.

Once the first coat is dry, you can apply more glaze to areas that need greater emphasis. Protect the finished result with a clear varnish.

CRACKING FINISHES

One of the cardinal rules of wood finishing is to avoid using incompatible finishes, but a purpose-made cracking varnish takes advantage of the different drying rates of oil-based and water-based finishes to create a most convincing aged surface. The required materials, usually known as ageing varnish and cracking varnish, are stocked by specialist suppliers.

Although the techniques are simple, perfect results rely on perfect timing, so a little experimentation pays dividends.

Preparation

To simulate crazed varnish, prepare the wood in the usual way, sealing the surface with a coat of matt acrylic varnish. Depending on the degree of ageing you want to suggest, you may want to apply a suitable wood stain beforehand.

To age existing paintwork, wash the surface to remove dirt and grease; rub down a gloss finish with wet-and-dry paper.

1 Applying ageing varnish

Paint a coat or ageing varnish onto the sealed or painted surface. Since the thickness of this initial coat determines how wide the final cracks will be, you can vary the effect by applying thicker varnish in those areas where you want to see more intense cracking.

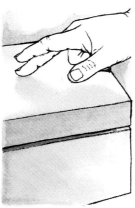

2 Timing the process

Leave the varnished workpiece in a warm atmosphere until it feels dry when you run a fingertip lightly across the surface; it should feel slightly tacky if you press hard. To apply cracking varnish before this stage will result in a wrinkled finish with only a minimal amount of cracking.

3 Applying cracking varnish

Paint an even coat of cracking varnish onto the workpiece and warm it gently with a hairdryer until the varnish begins to exhibit cracks, then leave the workpiece to dry hard in a warm room.

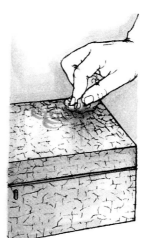

4 Emphasizing cracks

To simulate a discoloured crazed finish, rub artist's oil paint vigorously into the cracks, blending dark brown and black to create irregular colouring. Gently wipe paint from the surface to leave colour in the finer cracks. If the work is to be handled, apply a protective coat of oil varnish, but only after the artist's oil paint has dried thoroughly.

HEALTH AND SAFETY

Many wood finishes contain substances that are potentially harmful to your health, and some are also highly flammable. In addition to the following precautions, always observe manufacturers' instructions to protect yourself from health hazards and accidents when using or storing finishes.

Breathing solvent fumes
Breathing solvent vapours can be dangerous; if you begin to experience headaches, dizziness, fatigue or drowsiness, leave the workshop immediately.

If someone else feels faint, take them into fresh air, keeping them warm and at rest. Don't give him or her anything to eat or drink until fully recovered. If they are unconscious, put them in the recovery position and get urgent medical attention. If breathing has stopped, administer artificial ventilation (respiration).

• To protect yourself from solvent fumes, provide good natural ventilation when working with finishes; when spraying, fit an extractor in the spray booth.

• When it is impossible to provide adequate natural ventilation, and always when spraying substances, wear a gas-cartridge respirator. The filter can be changed to one that will protect you from wood dust when sanding.

Protecting your eyes
Wear goggles to protect your eyes from liquid splashes.

• If you get wood finishes or thinners in your eyes, flush them with running water for at least 10 minutes, holding your eyelids apart. If you wear contact lenses, remember to remove them first. Seek medical advice.

Skin contact
Repeated or prolonged contact with some wood finishes and thinners may lead to dermatitis. If in doubt, wear disposable gloves when applying finishes.

• Wash with soap and water or a proprietary skin cleanser; never use solvents or thinners to clean finishes from your skin.

Swallowing substances
If a child appears to have swallowed any wood finish or solvent, do not induce him or her to vomit. Keep the child calm and at rest, and obtain medical attention.

Fire precautions
Substances marked flammable should be handled and stored with care. Good ventilation is essential.

• Don't smoke in the workshop, and extinguish naked flames where workpieces are finished or left to dry.

• The fine mist created by spraying solvent finishes is highly flammable. It is important to install an explosion-proof (flame-proof) extractor fan, light fittings and switches in a spray booth.

• Sweep up shavings and dust regularly, and don't leave oil- or solvent-soaked rags in the workshop.

• Keep a fire extinguisher and fire blanket close at hand. Have the extinguisher checked regularly.

Storing finishes
If possible, store finishes and thinners in a locked shed or outhouse. If you need to transfer substances, label the containers clearly and avoid using food or drink cans or bottles that could be misidentified. Keep finish or solvent containers closed except when in use.

Disposing of substances
Don't pour solvents or finishes into drains or water courses. Contain and collect spills with a non-combustible absorbent material such as sand or earth.

• Ask your local authorities for advice on where and how to dispose safely of waste products, including empty containers.

See also:
Protecting yourself from dust, page 24.
Chemical strippers, page 32.
Bleaching wood, page 38.